MYSTERIOUS ❖ DEATHS

Amelia Earhart

These and other titles are included in the *Mysterious Deaths* series:

Butch Cassidy

Amelia Earhart

John F. Kennedy

Abraham Lincoln

The Little Princes in the Tower

Malcolm X

Marilyn Monroe

Mozart

MYSTERIOUS ■ DEATHS

Amelia Earhart

by Adam Woog

Lucent Books
P.O. Box 289011, San Diego, CA 92198-9011

Cover design by Carl Franzen

Library of Congress Cataloging-in-Publication Data

Woog, Adam, 1953-
    Amelia Earhart / by Adam Woog.
        p. cm.—(Mysterious deaths)
    Includes bibliographical references and index.
    ISBN 1-56006-261-4 (alk. paper)
    1. Earhart, Amelia, 1897–1937—Death and burial—Juvenile literature.
    2. Women air pilots—United States—Biography—Juvenile literature.
    I. Title.   II. Series.
    TL540.E3W663   1997
    629.13'092—dc20
    [B]   96–33399
                                                                          CIP
                                                                          AC

Printed in the U.S.A.
Copyright © 1997 by Lucent Books, Inc.
P.O. Box 289011, San Diego, CA 92198-9011

For Ralph Turman, who loves airplanes as much as he loves a good mystery

Contents

Foreword
Haunting Human History   8

Introduction
A Life in the Air   10

Chapter 1
Missing   22

Chapter 2
The Official Search   37

Chapter 3
The Rumors Begin   47

Chapter 4
How Did Earhart Die?   59

Chapter 5
Was Earhart a Spy?   76

Chapter 6
Was There a Government Cover-Up?   88

Epilogue
Amelia Lives   98

For Further Reading   105

Works Consulted   106

Index   108

Picture Credits   111

About the Author   112

Haunting Human History

The *Mysterious Deaths* series focuses on nine individuals whose deaths have never been fully explained. Some are figures from the distant past; others are far more contemporary. Yet all of them remain fascinating as much for who they were and how they lived as for how they died. Their lives were characterized by fame and fortune, tragedy and triumph, secrets that led to acute vulnerability. Our enduring fascination with these stories, then, is due in part to the lives of the victims and in part to the array of conflicting facts and opinions, as well as the suspense, that surrounds their deaths.

Some of the people profiled in the *Mysterious Deaths* series were controversial political figures who lived and died in the public eye. John F. Kennedy, Abraham Lincoln, and Malcolm X were all killed in front of crowds as guards paid to protect them were unable to stop their murders. Despite all precautions, their assassins found ample opportunity to carry out their crimes. In each case, the assassins were tried and convicted. So what remains mysterious? As the reader will discover, everything.

The two women in the series, Marilyn Monroe and Amelia Earhart, are equally well remembered. Both died at the heights of their careers; both, from all appearances, had everything to live for. Yet their deaths have also been shrouded in mystery. While there are simple explanations—Monroe committed suicide, Earhart's plane crashed—the public has never been able to accept them. The more researchers dig into the deaths, the more mysterious evidence they unearth. Monroe's predilection for affairs with prominent politicians may have led to her death. Earhart, brash and cavalier, may have been involved in a government plot that collapsed around her. And these theories do not exhaust the mysterious possibilities that continue to puzzle researchers.

The circumstances of the deaths of the remaining figures in the *Mysterious Deaths* series—Richard III's nephews Edward and

Richard; the brilliant composer Wolfgang Mozart; and the infamous bank robber Butch Cassidy—are less well known but no less fascinating.

For example, what are almost surely the skeletons of the little princes Edward and Richard were found buried at the foot of a stairway in the Tower of London in 1674. To many, the discovery proved beyond a doubt that their evil uncle, Richard III, murdered them to attain the throne. Yet others find Richard wrongly accused, the obvious scapegoat. The mysterious tale of their deaths—full of dungeons, plots, and treachery—is still intriguing today.

In the history books, Wolfgang Mozart died in poverty from a consumptive-like disease. Yet there are reports and rumors, snatches of information culled from distant records, that Mozart may have died from a slow poisoning. Who could have wanted to murder the famous composer? And why?

Finally, bank robber Butch Cassidy's death couldn't have been less mysterious—shot to death by military police in Bolivia along with his companion, the Sundance Kid. Then why did members of Butch Cassidy's family and numerous others swear to have seen him, in full health, in the United States years after his supposed death?

These true-life whodunits are filled with tantalizing "what ifs?" What if Kennedy had used the bulletproof plastic hood that his Secret Servicemen had ready? What if Lincoln had decided not to attend the theater—which he did only to please his wife? What if Monroe's friend, Peter Lawford, receiving no answer to his persistent calls, had gone to her house, as he wanted to do? These questions frustrate us as well as testify to a haunting aspect of human history—the way that seemingly insignificant decisions can alter its course.

A Life in the Air

Over the nine years spanning her first and last transoceanic flights, Amelia Earhart became one of the most famous women in the world. The private Amelia disliked that fame intensely. But the public Amelia played on it relentlessly as a platform on which to fight for her ideals of equality for women, international peace, and a world where flying would be commonplace, acceptable and accessible to all. She lived—and died—in dogged pursuit of her vision, and by so doing brought it even closer to reality.

Doris Rich, *Amelia Earhart*

Earhart was very much part of the history of modern America. She was an influential figure in the development of mass culture and the merchandizing of popular figures. She participated in the emergence of aviation as a major transportation industry. And she symbolized the new opportunities for women in modern life.

Susan Ware, *Still Missing: Amelia Earhart and the Search for Modern Feminism*

When I go, I would like to go in my plane. Quickly.

Amelia Earhart

Amelia Earhart was an unlikely prospect for fame. She was sickly as a child. Her adolescence was troubled. She drifted into adulthood with only vague ideas of her future. When she did become famous, she didn't much like it.

But Earhart soared to fame anyway. She was, and is, the world's most famous woman pilot. She was the first woman to cross the Atlantic by air and the second person to cross it alone. She set a number of other important aviation records. On the lecture circuit, she used her celebrity to speak out on controversial subjects such as pacifism and equal rights for women. She married a man who managed her career so that she remained in the spotlight, but she remained fiercely independent. At a time when American

The world's most famous woman pilot started out as a rather nondescript, unfocused teenager.

women had been able to vote for only a few years, Amelia Earhart was a strong, intelligent, and fearless role model.

People expected Earhart to spend her life speaking out, teaching, and flying for adventure and joy. But then she mysteriously vanished—and so became a legend.

Amelia Earhart's disappearance in the South Pacific in 1937, in the company of her navigator Fred Noonan, came during a daring attempt to make the first round-the-world flight at the equator. Earhart had planned to make it her last big flight. Her disappearance became one of the biggest news stories of the century. The largest sea-rescue mission in history was mounted, but no trace of the fliers was ever found. The years since have spawned countless theories about Earhart's fate—as well as ominous speculation about the real reasons for her final flight.

Amy and Edwin Earhart, Amelia's parents. Amelia's father's job required that the family be on the move constantly.

The possibilities seem endless. Perhaps Earhart was on a spy mission for the United States, seeking proof of Japan's military buildup prior to World War II. She may have been captured by the Japanese. If so, perhaps she was executed. One researcher claims that she returned to America under an assumed name. Several other researchers have charged that the U.S. and Japanese governments have conspired over decades to cover up the facts about the Earhart case.

On the other hand, perhaps A. E., as she liked to be called, was not a spy but simply an adventurer. Perhaps she just missed spotting the tiny island in the South Pacific that was her target. Perhaps Earhart and her copilot simply sank into the ocean.

The Flier Is Born

Amelia Mary Earhart was born on July 24, 1898, in the small town of Atchison, Kansas. Her athletic and strong-willed mother, Amy Otis Earhart, came from a prominent local family. Her tall, witty father, Edwin Earhart, was the son of a minister. Edwin worked as a claims adjuster for railroads, a job that required constant travel. Throughout Amelia's childhood, Amy, Amelia, and her younger sister Muriel followed Edwin around the Midwest or spent long periods living with Amy's father, a banker and judge.

Amelia was not strong as a child. She suffered from typhoid fever, diphtheria, and other serious diseases common in those days. But she survived and became a bright, curious, and mechanically minded child. In her memoirs, she recalls such childhood adventures as inventing a trap for chickens, taking daredevil sled rides with her sister, and building a huge backyard roller coaster out of scrap lumber.

Amelia first saw an airplane in 1908 at the Iowa State Fair, where she watched a pilot perform midair tricks in a crude biplane. The sight left her unimpressed. "It [the airplane] was a thing of rusty wire and wood," she later recalled. "I was much more interested in

Earhart, here at age six, was a sickly child who fell victim to several dangerous childhood diseases.

an absurd hat made of an inverted peach basket which I purchased for fifteen cents."

Aviation then was still a dangerous, untested, and very new adventure. Only a few years before, in 1903, Wilbur and Orville Wright had achieved the first successful flight of a manned, heavier-than-air craft. But pilots like Amelia Earhart would soon be blazing the trail for modern air travel.

The Flying Bug

Amelia's childhood was often difficult. Her father was an alcoholic. He had a violent temper when drunk, and he had trouble keeping a job. By the time Amelia was a teenager, the family broke up. Edwin moved to Kansas City; Amy and the girls went to Chicago, where Amy had friends. Amelia graduated from Hyde Park High School in Chicago in 1916. Unsure of her future, she went to Toronto, Canada, where her sister Muriel was in school.

Canada was already fighting in World War I. Amelia volunteered as a nurse's aide in a veteran's hospital until the war's end in November 1918. The sisters then moved to Northampton, Massachusetts, where Muriel attended Smith College and Amelia privately studied music and auto repair. Amelia subsequently moved to New York City and thought about attending Columbia University's medical school.

But her plans were cut short when her parents, temporarily back together and living in Los Angeles, asked her to join them.

A Part of History

In this passage from her book *Still Missing: Amelia Earhart and the Search for Modern Feminism,* sociologist Susan Ware comments on the important role Earhart played in American life, celebrity, aviation, and emerging roles for women:

"Earhart was very much part of the history of modern America. She was an influential figure in the development of mass culture and the merchandizing of popular figures. She participated in the emergence of aviation as a major transportation industry. And she symbolized the new opportunities for women in modern life."

Amelia as a volunteer nurse's aide during World War I. After high school graduation, Amelia moved in with her sister, Muriel.

Feeling that her presence might help their troubled relationship, she agreed. The move was fateful because it was in Los Angeles that Amelia caught the flying bug.

She was first attracted to the stunts performed by pilots who flew battered biplanes from a dusty airfield on Wilshire Boulevard in Los Angeles. In those days, there was no commercial aviation— no airlines, air cargo or mail. Instead, pilots made money by giving demonstration rides, teaching, and performing stunts. These daredevil pilots were called barnstormers; the nickname referred to the practice of flying from town to town and attracting attention by storming, or dive-bombing, a barn.

The twenty-three-year-old Amelia took a five-dollar ride in a plane. It was all she needed. As she often said later, after one look at the world from the air, she knew that aviation would be her greatest love.

Amelia stands with teacher Neta Snook (left) in front of a Kinner Airster biplane at a Los Angeles airport in 1920. Earhart sought out a female pilot to be her teacher.

She wrote in her memoirs that after the flight she tried to act nonchalant, knowing inside how important it was. "'I think I'd like to fly,' I told my family casually that evening, knowing full well I'd die if I didn't." In those days, an investment of five hundred dollars bought ten hours of lessons, enough to learn the basics of flight. Her father could not afford that much, so Amelia took a job at the phone company in order to pay the tuition.

She also found a woman pilot, Neta Snook, who agreed to teach her. Amelia already knew the importance of finding strong female role models. For years, she had been keeping a scrapbook of articles about accomplished women who held jobs as bank presidents, doctors, and fire lookouts.

The flying lessons were difficult and dangerous, but Amelia immediately took to the life of a pilot. She acquired the standard aviator's outfit: boots, khaki pants and shirt, scarf, knee-length leather jacket, and leather helmet with goggles. She even slept in her jacket to quickly give it a well-worn look. She also cut her hair short so that it fit snugly inside her helmet. She would retain this simple, practical style of dress and grooming all her life.

Within a year, Amelia was soloing—that is, flying by herself. When the Earharts sold their family house, Amy helped Amelia buy her first airplane: a second-hand, bright-yellow Kinner that she called the *Canary*. Amelia promptly used it to set a new woman's altitude record of fourteen thousand feet.

In 1924 Amelia's parents divorced. Amy and her daughters moved back East, and Amelia sold the plane to buy a car for the trip. She reenrolled at Columbia and flew rented planes whenever possible. During a summer break she worked at a Boston settlement house, helping newly arrived immigrants. She loved this job, and was considering a career in social work when fate again stepped in.

Lucky Lindy and Lady Lindy

In 1927 an unknown pilot named Charles Lindbergh captured the world's imagination by making the first nonstop solo air flight across the Atlantic Ocean. After his triumphant arrival in Paris, Charles Lindbergh instantly became Lucky Lindy, the world-famous aviator.

The following year, an American living in London organized a flight to give a woman a chance to fly the Atlantic. The pilot and mechanic would be paid for their work. An as-yet unchosen woman, officially the captain but really only a passenger, was expected to take part strictly for the adventure.

A panel of experts in America interviewed many contenders, but it chose Amelia. The panel members were favorably impressed by her intelligence, self-confidence, and straightforward manner. She, in turn, was delighted. As she wrote to a friend, "When a great adventure's offered you—you don't refuse it, that's all."

The flight was hard and perilous and a huge success. Exactly twenty hours and forty minutes after leaving Newfoundland in northeast Canada, pilot Bill Stultz, mechanic Slim Gordon, and captain Amelia Earhart landed in a remote field in Wales, in the west of England. Lindbergh had been greeted by an immense, cheering crowd when he touched down in Paris; when Earhart landed, she saw only a handful of startled farmers.

Once the British press found her, however, she was thrust into the international spotlight. Stultz and Gordon, who had done the work and deserved recognition as well, were virtually ignored in favor of the more newsworthy and photogenic Earhart. She was showered with attention in England, on her return to America by ship, and long after.

Everyone wanted to see, meet, or interview "Lady Lindy," the name given to her by a fond public and press. She did, in fact, bear a remarkable physical resemblance to Lindbergh. Both fliers had the same freckled coloring, the same rangy build, the same shy smile, and the same quiet self-assurance. But Earhart hated the nickname, which she thought was insulting to both her and Lindbergh.

Meeting George Putnam

One of Earhart's admirers was George Palmer Putnam, grandson of the founder of the publishing firm G. P. Putnam's. Putnam had published Lindbergh's book about his flight and had been on the panel that selected Earhart for the transatlantic flight. A wizard at public relations, Putnam now arranged to become her manager and agent. He also published a book she wrote about her grand adventure.

Earhart's fame and accomplishments grew. She bought another airplane and flew solo from New York to California and back, thus becoming the first woman pilot to make a coast-to-coast return flight. Putnam arranged a series of high-paying product endorsements, writing assignments, and lecture tours for his client. Earhart also competed in the first Women's Air Derby—Santa Monica, California, to Cleveland, Ohio, in eight days. Several of the contestants were more skilled and experienced than Earhart, and she finished only third out of twenty. Thanks to Putnam's publicity efforts, however, she was the race's undisputed star.

Marriage and Solo Flight

Earhart and Putnam became increasingly close as he managed her career. Eventually, Putnam divorced his wife in the hopes that his famous client would marry him. He proposed six times before she accepted. One day in 1930, while waiting for her airplane to warm up, she finally said yes. Then she patted Putnam's arm and flew away.

The marriage was unusual for its time. Both partners were celebrities. Both were strong willed, driven, and determined to succeed. Earhart clearly knew she was the equal of any man and, unlike many women in the 1930s, was not afraid to show it. Right from the beginning, the couple made all decisions—from small domestic matters to life-changing flight plans—together.

The crew of the Friendship *waves to crowds in front of city hall. From left to right are pilot Bill Stultz, Amelia Earhart, and Slim Gordon. Amelia did not feel she deserved the title "first woman to fly the Atlantic," since she did not pilot the flight.*

Some biographers feel that Putnam manipulated his wife's career, forcing her to maintain an exhausting, breakneck work pace. But Earhart was as strong willed and motivated as her husband. Doris Rich, in her biography *Amelia Earhart*, wrote that the two clearly needed each other:

No other woman pilot had the necessary combination of courage, intelligence, looks, and charm. No other was so obsessed with showing the world that women were the equals of men. Certainly no other woman aviator had the patience and self-esteem required to be Putnam's wife and business partner.

Earhart after participating in the 1929 Women's Air Derby with fellow fliers Gladys O'Donell (third from left), and Louise Thaden (fifth from right).

Earhart herself once described her marriage in aviation terms as "a reasonable partnership . . . conducted under a satisfactory system of dual control." According to Elinor Smith, also a pioneer female aviator, Earhart's reluctance to take center stage was both a calculated public relations move and an indication of her character. "The image of a shy and retiring individual thrust against her will into the public eye was a figment of Putnam's lively imagination," she once remarked. In a reference to the flamboyant prizefighter, Smith added, "Amelia was about as shy as Muhammad Ali."

A Career Develops

Earhart had always regretted that the transatlantic crossing on which she was captain made her famous, even though she had done none of the actual work. She decided, therefore, to make the trip again—this time by herself. The publicity and outpouring of public affection for Earhart after this fifteen-hour adventure in May 1932 was even greater than before. She was greeted by royalty in England, ecstatic ticker-tape parades in America, and even a telegram from her dry cleaner: "Knew you would do it. I never lose a customer."

In the next few years, Earhart's career continued to soar. She wrote another book. She became close friends with President Franklin D. Roosevelt and his wife, Eleanor. She continued to speak out regularly on her favorite topics, and she continued to set new flight records: a New York to Los Angeles speed record, the first flight ever from Hawaii to California, the first solo flight from Los Angeles to Mexico City. She was the first woman to fly an autogiro (a cross between an airplane and a helicopter) and the first to cross America nonstop.

She also accepted an offer from Purdue University in Lafayette, Indiana, to counsel female students and conduct research in aviation. The university bought her a new airplane: a twin-engine Lockheed Electra 10E, the biggest, fastest, most powerful craft she had ever flown. Earhart formally accepted the plane on July 24, 1936, her thirty-eighth birthday. Officially a research vessel to be used in studying long-term flight, the plane cost about eighty thousand dollars—roughly a million and a half dollars in today's money.

Earhart would fly this plane to her final destination.

Missing

Please know I am quite aware of the hazards. I want to do it because I want to do it. Women must try to do things as men have tried. When they fail, their failure must be but a challenge to others.

Amelia Earhart, in a letter to George Palmer Putnam
before one of her long-distance flights

Earhart decided that she would fly her new airplane around the world. She was not the first to plan an around-the-world flight when she began preparations in 1936. Two other aviators had already succeeded. Her journey, however, would be different.

For one thing, no woman had attempted it. Also, the other pilots had taken routes that were relatively far north. Earhart planned to stay close to the equator. This route would make her journey, at about twenty-seven thousand miles, the longest single air flight ever. It was also much more dangerous than the other flights, since it involved longer stretches of travel over open seas.

Earhart planned to travel westward, from Oakland, California, to Hawaii, Australia, the Middle East, Africa, Brazil, and back to Oakland in about a month. She and Putnam spent nearly a year preparing for the flight. Earhart practiced with the new plane while Putnam took care of the complex travel arrangements, such as stockpiling spare parts and fuel in remote locations and obtaining formal permission to land in various countries. The Electra, meanwhile, was modified extensively with special glass in the windows to allow distortion-free navigating by the stars and extra-large fuel tanks that filled most of the cabin space.

As always Earhart needed to generate large amounts of money to cover her expenses. Putnam proved masterful at creating publicity for his wife and found sponsors and other cash sources for her. One fund-raising method involved having Earhart autograph thousands of air-mail envelopes, called cachets, which she would mail home from points on the trip then sell to the public.

New York *Herald-Tribune* reporter Carl Allen recalled that at a breakfast shortly before her departure, Putnam took away Earhart's orange juice and handed her a stack of envelopes. "Don't forget our agreement, darling," Putnam said. He explained to the reporter that his wife had to sign ten envelopes before she could have juice, fifteen more before breakfast, and twenty-five more before bed at night. With this schedule, Earhart was able to leave with over six thousand signed envelopes in her cargo hold.

It was exhausting work, but finally all the details fell into place. Earhart left Oakland for Hawaii on March 17, 1937, accompanied by navigator Harry Manning. Manning was an experienced sea captain but had limited experience with aerial navigation, so another navigator, Fred Noonan, planned to travel with them as far as Australia.

Earhart poses with the Electra 10E bought for her by Purdue University. Soon after receiving the plane, Earhart planned to fly around the world.

The trip to Hawaii was uneventful, but then disaster struck. During the takeoff for the next leg of the trip, the plane went out of control while taxiing on the ground. No one was hurt, but the Electra was damaged. The plane needed two months of repair work at the Lockheed factory in California before Earhart could fly it again.

Preparing for a Second Try

Back in California, Putnam and Earhart pressed forward with plans for a second try. Several major changes were necessary. Because of changes in seasonal weather patterns, the flight's direction would have to be eastward. Also, Manning bowed out because of previous commitments, and Noonan stepped in as the full-time navigator.

The preparations went ahead despite some concerns over Earhart's health and abilities. Paul Mantz, Earhart's flying coach and later a top Hollywood stunt pilot, believed that she was on the

A *Home for Birds Once Again*

In his book *The Search for Amelia Earhart*, CBS radio newsman Fred Goerner remarks that Earhart's sudden disappearance signaled the end of the airstrip on Howland. The navy had built this and similar facilities on Jarvis and Baker Islands to test potential Pacific air routes. Goerner wrote: "When the Electra failed to arrive at Howland that July

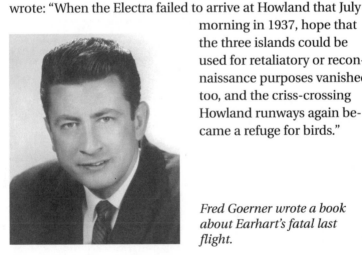

morning in 1937, hope that the three islands could be used for retaliatory or reconnaissance purposes vanished too, and the criss-crossing Howland runways again became a refuge for birds."

Fred Goerner wrote a book about Earhart's fatal last flight.

Amelia poses with (from left to right) Paul Mantz, Harry Manning, and Fred Noonan at a press conference to announce her plans to fly around the world.

edge of exhaustion before she even took off. She had been driving herself too hard for too long: preparing for the flight, recovering from a sinus operation, overseeing construction of a California home for her and Putnam, and maintaining a nonstop schedule of lectures and endorsements.

Al Bresnik, the photographer Putnam hired to document the project, suggested another reason for Earhart's fatigue. He said that Earhart told him before the flight that she thought she was pregnant. The notes she made during her journey do mention nausea, which she thought was caused by gas leaks but which could have been morning sickness.

Meanwhile, some people expressed concern that Earhart's skills were inadequate. Mantz thought she needed more practice with the plane's power settings in order to create the best fuel consumption ratios for various weather conditions. He also thought she was poorly trained in the use of her life raft, flare gun, and other emergency equipment.

Paul Mantz (left) and Amelia pose in front of the Lockheed Electra she would use in her last flight. Mantz often disagreed with Earhart on the amount of equipment and experience that were required for the flight.

A radio expert who worked with her, Joseph Gurr, later said he thought her radio equipment and training were very poor. Gurr said she was "too casual" in her approach to communications and did not think she was paying enough attention to basic skills. "We never covered actual operations," he said, "such as taking a bearing with a direction finder, not even contacting another radio station."

Earhart made other questionable decisions in the weeks before the flight. Mantz wanted her to carry a 250-foot trailing wire, which would give direction-finding equipment on land enough time to "fix," or locate, her position. But the wire, which had to be reeled in and out every time the plane was airborne, was heavy and cumbersome. Feeling that its usefulness did not justify the weight and trouble, Earhart left it behind.

Earhart also rejected two other basic pieces of radio equipment—a Morse code key and a 500-kilocycle (kilohertz) radio. Neither Earhart nor Noonan had much experience with Morse, so the key would do them little good. As for the radio, Earhart decided to rely entirely on voice broadcasts on two higher frequencies, 6210 kilocycles in the day and 3105 kilocycles at night.

In addition, although the Electra series of airplanes maintained a good service record, Earhart's plane had its share of problems. Before a race in 1936, its oil seals leaked and the hatch blew off. Later, both engines, one after the other, had caught fire while warming up for takeoff. Earhart also had recurrent trouble with crucial parts like the propeller bearings, shock absorbers, oil lines, and fuel-flow gauge. However, Earhart and Putnam ignored these and other problems as the departure date grew closer.

Around the World

The Electra was finally repaired and Earhart flew it from Oakland, California, to Miami, Florida, on May 22. With her were Putnam, Noonan, and a mechanic, Bo McKneely. This flight was the actual start of the journey, but Putnam wanted to heighten the publicity value by building suspense. He called it a shakedown cruise and denied to the press that the real trip had begun.

Apparently, Earhart was ready to make this adventure her last big flight. She told a reporter in Miami that this trip would be her final try for a record flight. She was nearly forty, she pointed out, and wanted "to make way for the younger generation before I'm feeble, too." In the future, she said, she would stick to flying for research and for fun.

Earhart and Noonan took off from Miami on June 1. The plan was to fly around the world and back to Oakland by the Fourth of July—a very tight schedule. Earhart was being pressured to travel quickly, largely because Putnam had lined up lectures, book contracts, and other commitments for his famous wife.

The Electra flew without incident to Puerto Rico and South America, and then across the Atlantic to Africa. Earhart's often hasty approach to decision making, however, became evident when they hit the African coast. Noonan said that their intended target city of Dakar, French West Africa (now Senegal), was to the south. Earhart ignored his advice. Instead, she flew north for 50 miles until she spotted another town, which she knew was 160 miles north of Dakar. She was forced to turn around and fly south to reach Dakar.

On they traveled across Africa, the Middle East, and Southeast Asia. All along the way, they battled tropical rainstorms, strong headwinds, and other hardships.

The Electra was flying well, but it was noisy and uncomfortable both for Earhart in the cramped cockpit and for Noonan at his chart table in the cabin. The roar of the engines was so loud that the only way they could communicate with each other was by passing notes with a fishing pole.

The fliers experienced other hardships as well. On land, they slept on bug-infested mattresses in oppressively hot airfield barracks. Another problem was the possible contamination of stored fuel. At each stop, this fuel had to be carefully strained through special cloth filters. In the Sahara Desert, where daytime temperatures usually hover around 100° Fahrenheit in summer, refueling took place after dark to avoid gas explosions on the hot metal of the airplane.

Earhart and Noonan (back to camera) have lunch with airport employees in Caripito, Venezuela, the second stop on her around-the-world flight.

They flew across the Red and Arabian Seas and on to Pakistan, then a part of British India. They were constantly rushing. In her journal, which she mailed to Putnam in segments as she wrote it, Earhart noted, "Push through, we're always pushing through, hurrying on our long way, trying to get some other place instead of enjoying the place we'd already got to. . . . Sometime I hope to stay somewhere as long as I like."

In India, they stopped to repair a broken fuel analyzer. On the next leg, en route to Burma, they encountered rains so heavy that the paint on the Electra's wings was beaten off.

On the island of Java, mechanics overhauled the plane while Earhart and Noonan rested. They had covered over twenty thousand miles in 135 hours of flight time, all in less than a month. They had made thirty stops in nineteen countries on five continents. For twenty-one nights they had slept in primitive accommodations and brutal heat. Earhart had battled bouts of nausea and diarrhea. Still, after a few days of rest, she and Noonan pressed on.

Stopover at Lae

Lae, New Guinea, is the last place where Amelia Earhart and Fred Noonan were, without a doubt, seen alive.

Their stay at Lae was extended a few days because of bad weather. Several airport personnel and government officials who met the fliers later remarked that Noonan, who had a reputation as a serious drinker but who had given it up before the flight, was drinking again. Noonan also complained to dinner companions one night that Earhart was pushing too hard—or was being pushed.

The navigator had his work cut out for him on this next leg of the journey, the most dangerous of the entire trip. It required a long haul over open water, with no identifying landmarks, to Howland Island, where the U.S. Coast Guard vessel *Itasca* was waiting for them. If the weather turned overcast or stormy, he would not be able to set a course by the stars, the most accurate means of navigation. His backup methods, including use of such instruments as a chronometer and gyroscope, were unreliable and had been giving him trouble all along.

Even his basic information was incorrect. Noonan's chart, the most accurate at the time, showed Howland as lying seven miles northwest of its actual location. (The error was discovered by later mapping.) Finally, he was shooting for an incredibly difficult target, one tiny speck in a vast ocean. As biographer Doris Rich put it, "Even if Noonan was not drinking he faced a formidable task in locating a sand bar in the mid-Pacific that was two miles long and three-quarters of a mile wide, with a maximum elevation of twenty-five feet."

Earhart worried about Noonan's drinking, about the equipment, and about herself. She sent her husband a cable, which some sources say referred to "personnel unfitness." Others quote it as "crew unfitness." Although this reference is probably to Noonan's drinking, Earhart may have been referring to her own fatigue.

Nevertheless, she was determined to press on. As Doris Rich noted, "[I]f pride and willpower could not get her to Howland, they could not permit her to turn back." She invited Harry Balfour, a New Guinea Airways radio operator stationed at Lae, to accompany them to Howland. Apparently, she extended the invitation either because she wanted Balfour to keep an eye on Noonan or because she realized they needed more radio expertise—or both. In any case, Balfour declined.

Worried about the weight of the aircraft, Earhart and Noonan had long since jettisoned any equipment that was not essential. Every spare inch of space and pound of weight was crucial to maximize their precious load of fuel. They also left their parachutes at Lae, reasoning that they would be useless in the middle of the ocean. According to later testimony by Harry Balfour, at the last minute they even unloaded some of their survival equipment, including a raft and a flare pistol used for making distress signals.

Final Departure

Earhart and Noonan were finally able to leave when the weather cleared on July 2, Lae time. (Howland and Lae are on opposite sides of the international date line, so the date was still July 1 on Howland Island.) They expected the trip to take about eighteen hours. The Electra had a full load of fuel, about one thousand gallons for the 2,556-mile trip to Howland. This amount of fuel gave the fliers roughly twenty hours of flight time, depending on weather conditions and how wisely Earhart conserved fuel.

There is some conflict about exactly how much fuel the Electra was carrying. Full capacity was 1,150 gallons, but Earhart was worried that the Electra would not become airborne with too heavy a load. Noonan told a reporter on the night before departure that

A Possibly Fatal Mistake

The area of the Pacific over which Earhart and Noonan were flying was very poorly charted. In fact, a possibly fatal charting error may have been responsible for Noonan's inability to navigate safely to Howland. Unfortunately, the error was discovered too late to help him. According to the standard reference work used at the time, Lippincott's *Geographical Dictionary of the World*, Howland Island was located at latitude 0 degrees 49'00 north, longitude 176 degrees 43'09 west. This measurement was considered correct as of the spring of 1937 when Earhart's colleague Clarence Williams used it to draw the original flight plan for her.

A year before, however, a navigational patrol mission had corrected this measurement to latitude 0 degrees 48'00 north, longitude 176 degrees 38'12 west. This small but significant change had not yet made its way into print when Williams prepared his flight plan. The difference amounted to just under six miles—a crucial difference.

By following knowledge presumed correct when charting Earhart's route, colleague Clarence Williams may have made a fatal error.

they would have 950 gallons. A mechanic who worked on the plane and New Guinea's superintendent of civil aviation both stated later that the fliers left with 1,100 gallons.

Even with less than a completely full load, eyewitnesses reported that the Electra barely lifted off the ground. The plane lumbered down the runway and disappeared off the cliff at the end of the island runway. For a heart-stopping moment, those observing the takeoff feared that the plane would fall into the ocean. The Electra did, in fact, come so close to the water's surface that its propellers threw sea spray into the air. But the heavy plane finally took off and soon was out of sight.

Radioman Harry Balfour stayed in touch with Earhart for the next seven hours from his post on Lae. After that, he heard nothing from Earhart but ominous silence. The plane was due to pass over the ship *Ontario*, which was stationed halfway between Lae and Howland. On board, three men were keeping a visual watch, and a radio operator was listening and broadcasting regular signals. But Earhart was neither seen nor heard by the *Ontario* as she made her way to Howland.

Crossed Signals

This failure to communicate was partly caused by muddled information about the nature of Earhart's radio capabilities.

Serious miscommunications developed from the beginning among Earhart, Putnam (who was at the Coast Guard station in San Francisco), Richard Black of the Department of the Interior (Putnam's representative aboard the *Itasca*), and Commander Warner K. Thompson (captain of the *Itasca* and head of the communications network set up for Earhart). For instance, Putnam apparently thought that a 500-kilocycle radio was aboard the Electra, and he told Thompson incorrectly that Earhart would be broadcasting some of the time on that frequency.

Her equipment, meanwhile, was incompatible with the radios aboard the *Ontario* and the *Itasca*. The *Ontario*'s range was too low for her to hear without the trailing aerial she had left behind in Miami. The *Itasca* had a direction finder, but it too required the trailing wire. A second direction finder—an experimental high-frequency model—had been set up on Howland Island. However, it needed strong signals at least two minutes long, and Earhart never made a broadcast that long.

The information about the available range of frequencies was also confusing. From San Francisco, Putnam assured the *Itasca* that Earhart's range was 200 to 1500 kilocycles and 2400 to 4800 kilocycles, but he also suggested using the more reliable lower range. Earhart, meanwhile, cabled Thompson that she would broadcast by voice only on 3105 kilocycles. Putnam also said she would be broadcasting on a regular schedule. In fact, she did not signal regularly at any stage.

At one point after establishing contact with the *Itasca*, Earhart asked the ship's radio crew to transmit at 7500 kilocycles. This request made little sense to them. Perhaps, with her limited knowledge of radio, she had confused 7500 kilocycles with 400 kilocycles—the equivalent of 750.00 meters, a standard direction-finding frequency. The confusion was as basic as a modern-day radio listener trying to tune in an AM radio station by using a number on the FM band.

The end result was that only one frequency—3105 kilocycles—was open to Earhart. She could both send and receive on that frequency alone. This higher frequency was not as reliable or clear as a lower one would have been.

Pilots in the early days of aviation generally distrusted technology and preferred to use their own instincts. Earhart shared this attitude, referring to her new equipment at one point in her journal as "pretty sissy." She apparently felt that voice communication on one frequency would be sufficient—a notion that was tragically wrong. As Commander Thompson noted in a later report, "Viewed from the fact that Miss Earhart's flight was largely dependent on radio communication, her attitude towards [communications] arrangements was casual to say the least."

The Last Messages

A perfect day had dawned on Howland Island on July 2nd. Offshore, the *Itasca* was waiting. The ship's searchlights had been lit all night, and as morning broke her smokestacks began to pour out dark smoke to mark the way. Chief Radioman Leo G. Bellarts, his crew, two newspaper reporters, Commander Thompson, various government officials, and the rest of the ship's crew were standing by.

At midnight Howland time, about six and a half hours before Earhart's scheduled arrival, the ship's radio crew had begun broadcasting weather and homing signals on the half hour. At 2:45 A.M.

Earhart lost radio contact and disappeared on July 3, 1937. No one has ever been able to determine what happened to the missing pilot.

they finally heard from her. She announced calmly that the weather was "cloudy and overcast." The rest of her transmission was lost in heavy static.

The *Itasca* continued to send signals but heard nothing more from Earhart until 3:45 when the ship received this message: "*Itasca* from Earhart. . . . *Itasca* from Earhart. . . . Overcast. . . . Will listen on hour and half hour on 3105. . . . Will listen on hour and half hour on 3105." The *Itasca* sent another message on its regular schedule, but Earhart did not acknowledge it.

Just before 5:00 A.M., Earhart broke in to the *Itasca's* scheduled broadcast. The crew could hear her voice, but only the words "partly cloudy" could be understood above the static.

Radio Troubles

At 6:15, fifteen minutes before her scheduled arrival, Earhart asked the *Itasca* to take a bearing on her and said she'd whistle into the microphone to help the direction finders. But her signal was too brief, and static nearly drowned out what could be heard. Half an hour later, she said she was about one hundred miles out, but did not stay on the air long enough for the *Itasca* to get a bearing. Apparently, Earhart could not hear the ship's signals, including the crew's requests for lengthier broadcasts.

No further word from Earhart until 7:42 A.M. Then she said, "We must be on you, but cannot see you. But gas is running low. Been unable to reach you by radio. We are flying at altitude 1,000 feet." The *Itasca* crew heard this broadcast clearly, an indication that the plane was probably close. According to the second radioman's log, Earhart also stated that she had only half an hour of fuel remaining. Commander Thompson later stated that Earhart's voice was starting to sound distraught and worried.

At 7:58 she signaled again, using her radio call letters: "KHAQQ calling *Itasca.* We are circling, but cannot hear you. Go ahead on 7500 either now or on scheduled time of half hour." The ship sent out a long signal. Earhart replied, "We are receiving your signals, but are unable to get a minimum. Please take a bearing on us and answer with voice on 3105." Again she whistled, but again she was lost in static. Apparently, she still couldn't hear the messages from the *Itasca.*

Then, at 8:45 A.M., the ship received the final message from Amelia Earhart: "We are on line of position 157 dash 337. Will repeat this message on 6210 kilocycles. Wait, listening on 6210 kilocycles. We are running north and south."

This message puzzled the *Itasca* radio crew. The phrase *line of position* was unclear. The radiomen assumed she was talking about a longitudinal reading, which would specify a line of longitude. These lines are imaginary north-south lines running around the earth that help navigators find their positions. The corresponding east-west lines are called lines of latitude.

Earhart seemed to know which north-south line she was on, but not which east-west line. Since she was unable to get a latitudinal reading, she could not locate her exact position. Apparently, when she said that she was "running north and south," she meant that she was flying north and south along "line of position 157 dash 337," looking for Howland Island.

In any case, the *Itasca* crew was concerned about Earhart's shifting use of frequencies. Radioman Bellarts replied, "*Itasca* to KHAQQ. We heard you okay on 3105 kilocycles. Please stay on 3105, do not hear you on 6210."

There was no response.

By this time, Thompson knew that he had a genuine emergency. The Electra's fuel would soon be gone. The batteries used to power the direction finder on Howland Island were exhausted. Radio messages to Earhart were apparently not getting through. And there was no guarantee the *Itasca* would hear from her again.

He decided it was time to start looking for the famous flyer.

2 *The Official Search*

Amelia's neglect of so vital an element as telegraph-radio originated in her own nature and past experiences. In spite of her denials she was a romantic about flight. It was a near-transcendent experience for her and she instinctively avoided the communication that broke her isolation from the earthbound and mundane.

Doris Rich, *Amelia Earhart*

Thompson began to try to determine the Electra's location. He knew, for one thing, that the fliers were exhausted. Earhart and Noonan had been awake for more than twenty-four hours and airborne in a noisy, cramped, rattling plane for at least twenty of those hours. In their fatigued state, they could easily have made a mistake and headed seriously off course.

Nevertheless, based on what she had said and her relatively strong signals, Earhart was probably close to her target. Thompson reasoned that she was near Howland and in stormy weather. Earhart had stated she was flying at an altitude of only one thousand feet. The only reason to fly so low was to avoid clouds. (Visibility was better at a higher elevation, so she would be higher if possible.) Another clue that Earhart was in stormy weather was the heavy static accompanying her messages.

The weather was clear around Howland and to the south and east, but the area to the north and west was covered with heavy clouds. Based on this logic, then, the plane was either to the north, west, or northwest. Also, Earhart's last message referred to a "line of position 157 dash 337." Thompson assumed she was referring to a sun line. Therefore, Thomson believed that the fliers were either north or south of Howland and, unsure of their position, were running that line, that is, flying back and forth along it.

Confusion About Radio Equipment

About six months after Earhart's disappearance, the Coast Guard Division at San Francisco issued its official report on the matter, which remained classified until the 1960s. It stated, in part: "To this day, no one in the Coast Guard has been able to find out exactly what radio equipment Miss Earhart did have aboard. Even Mr. Putnam in San Francisco was very badly informed about flight schedules and actual conditions on the plane. Miss Earhart knew the *Itasca* carried a low-frequency direction finder, but she never broadcast on 500 [kilocycles] for a bearing and she never chose to explain why not."

In the opinion of biographer Mary Love, Noonan may have deliberately directed Earhart to a point slightly north of Howland. When Noonan estimated that the plane was at a point in the ocean due north of Howland Island, he would then have told Earhart to head south. Love speculated in her book, *The Sound of Wings*, that Earhart disregarded Noonan when he told her to change direction after hours of traveling in the same direction. Instead, she preferred to rely on her pilot's intuition. Referring to the incident in Africa when Earhart had doubted Noonan, Love wrote, "Everything indicates that it was a reliance on her own similar instinct that led her to ignore Noonan's navigational instruction on the flight to Dakar."

In any case, Thompson estimated that Earhart had enough fuel to last until about 10:00 A.M. When that time came and went with no signal from her, he sent a cable to George Putnam at the Coast Guard headquarters in San Francisco:

> WILL COMMENCE SEARCH IN NORTHWEST QUADRANT FROM HOWLAND AS MOST PROBABLE AREA. . . . UNDERSTAND SHE WILL FLOAT FOR A LIMITED TIME.

The largest sea-rescue mission in history was under way.

Chances of Survival

Assuming that Earhart and Noonan crashed in the open sea, people immediately began to debate how long they might have survived.

Could they have even lived through the initial landing? Paul Mantz had given Earhart instructions on ditching an airplane at sea, but she had never actually done it. If the plane was out of fuel, she would have had to make a dead-stick landing—that is, gliding down without the control provided by engine power. A dead-stick landing is a difficult job even in the smoothest conditions. According to the *Itasca's* official report, the seas were turbulent on July 2 with waves four to six feet high. Even if she had been able to use power to put the plane down, calculating the Electra's height above

Could Earhart have survived an emergency landing in the open sea? Many experts think not.

the water would have been difficult. If she stalled the engines and began her landing too high, the impact would have killed or seriously wounded them both. A damaged plane, furthermore, would have sunk in seconds.

Earhart had no shoulder harness. Directly in front of her on the control panel was a radio receiver housed in a sharp-cornered metal box. If the impact had been great, she likely would have hit her head on it. Noonan would have been in his section of the cabin or in the copilot's chair at the time of impact. In either case, he would also have had minimal protection.

Even if Earhart put the plane down perfectly, the chances of survival were not great. The Electra would have floated nose down and tail up because of the weight of the engines and the buoyancy of the empty fuel tanks in the rear. The cockpit hatch would have been underwater. To reach the escape hatch in the rear, the fliers would have had to climb almost straight up, clambering awkwardly over the extra fuel tanks.

Harry Balfour, the radio operator in Lae, testified later that Earhart and Noonan left their raft and other emergency equipment behind. Even if the raft was still aboard, it would have been in a rear cabin bulkhead. Earhart and Noonan would have had to pull it from above their heads, partially inflate it with a carbon dioxide canister, open the hatch, throw the raft into the water, jump after it,

Radio Transmission

Pilots choose their radio equipment and frequencies for use in a variety of situations. When communicating by radio, some frequencies are better than others under certain circumstances. Time of day or night, weather conditions, and land or sea formations can all affect transmission on a given frequency.

For instance, radio signals travel farther at night because changes in the ionization of the earth's atmosphere affect its ability to reflect radio waves. For the same reason, lower frequencies are more effective at night than in the daytime.

These frequencies are measured in an increment that in Earhart's time was called a kilocycle but that is now also referred to as a kilohertz.

President Franklin Delano Roosevelt ordered a massive search effort after hearing of Earhart's disappearance.

and finish inflating it before they could climb in. At least ten forced landings on water have occurred in airplanes identical to Earhart's. According to reports from these accidents, Earhart and Noonan would have had about eight minutes in which to evacuate with the raft before their plane sank beneath the waves.

Even if the fliers survived a crash landing in the ocean and made it into the raft, their troubles would have been far from over. Supplies of food and water were limited. Their ability to avoid sunstroke and dehydration was minimal. In addition, sharks were a constant danger in those waters.

The Search Goes On

Once Thompson sounded the alarm, the full force of the U.S. military was brought into action. President Roosevelt ordered all available ships, planes, and personnel to help find his missing friend. In addition to the *Itasca* and the *Ontario*, the search team included some four thousand men aboard ships including a battleship, four destroyers, a minesweeper, a seaplane tender, and an aircraft carrier.

The Itasca, *one of the ships sent out to search for Earhart and her plane.*

Some members of Congress protested the cost of the search—a quarter of a million dollars a day, some four million dollars in all, an enormous sum by the day's standards. Roosevelt's critics accused him of abusing his power to rescue a friend. Roosevelt replied that military ships and airplanes needed to perform practice searches anyway, and there was no reason why such maneuvers should not have a practical end.

In America and elsewhere, the disappearance of Amelia Earhart made immediate headlines. In fact, it would prove to be one of the ten most reported news stories of the century. The entire world waited breathlessly for word from the remote South Pacific.

Were the fliers still alive? If so, several possibilities emerged as to their location. They could have been with the Electra, still afloat on empty fuel tanks. They could have been in a raft. They could have been picked up by one of the Japanese fishing boats that sailed regularly in the area. Or they could have turned back in desperation to find an island—possibly one of the Gilbert Islands—that might have provided a safe haven.

Friends, family, and military personnel who were with George Putnam in San Francisco during this period later described him as

Out in Time for Christmas

A leading aviation navigator of the 1930s, Bradford Washburn, was one of the first people approached about being the navigator for Earhart's around-the-world flight. He declined the trip, however, when he discovered that Earhart did not plan to use what he considered adequate radio equipment. He felt that proper communications equipment was only one of many things that Earhart was sacrificing in favor of speed.

Quoted in Susan Ware's book *Still Missing*, Washburn recalled a preflight conversation with Earhart and Putnam about the possibility of installing radio equipment on Howland Island that would help ground crews communicate with Earhart. Putnam turned to Earhart and said, "If we have to get radio equipment all the way out there, there wouldn't be any chance of getting your book out for the Christmas sale [season]."

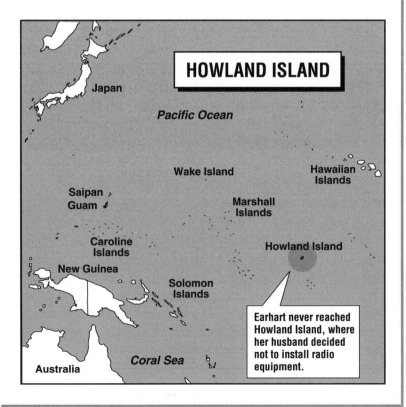

HOWLAND ISLAND

Japan

Pacific Ocean

Wake Island

Hawaiian Islands

Saipan
Guam

Marshall Islands

Caroline Islands

Howland Island

New Guinea

Solomon Islands

Australia

Coral Sea

Earhart never reached Howland Island, where her husband decided not to install radio equipment.

distraught. He was constantly wondering what more could be done and then rushing off to organize it. Noonan's wife, who joined Putnam at one point, remembered him pacing for hours in his shirtsleeves, perspiration streaming from his face. Publicly, though, he remained confident. He told a reporter for the New York *Sunday Mirror*, "A. E. will pull through. She has more courage than anyone I know. I am worried, of course, but I have confidence in her ability to handle any situation."

He continued to hold out the prospect that Earhart and Noonan would be found. For one thing, he apparently did not know that she had ditched most of her survival equipment. Looking back, this optimism seems touchingly desperate and naive; at one point, he sent a radiogram to the naval search headquarters at Pearl Harbor in Hawaii that read, "If they are down, they can stay afloat indefinitely. Their empty tanks will give them buoyancy. Besides, they have all the emergency equipment they'll need—everything."

Keeping a Vigil

Amelia's mother, Amy, also remained confident that her daughter would soon be found. Speaking to reporters at her home in Los Angeles, she responded to a question about Amelia's safety with a firm, "No, no, no! No, of course not. I know she's all right. I know she will soon be found. I know she is alive." For the next two years, in fact, Amy Earhart kept a suitcase packed with clothes, sunburn cream, hair scissors, and other supplies in case she received sudden word that her daughter was safe.

On July 7 Eleanor Roosevelt devoted her nationally syndicated weekly newspaper column to her friend. She wrote:

> I feel sure that if she comes through safely she will feel that what she has learned makes it all worth while. But her friends will wish science could be served without so much risk to a fine person whom many people love as a person and not as a pilot or adventurer.

As the days wore on, however, the chances of finding Earhart grew steadily slimmer. Putnam became more and more distraught. After reports that he had suffered a breakdown were made public, Putnam hastily issued a denial, telling reporters, "I have not collapsed. I have indulged in no public sobbing. . . . If Amelia is dead it is the way she would have chosen."

Earhart's disappearance galvanized public sympathy. Eleanor Roosevelt dedicated her nationally syndicated column to the subject.

While Putnam and the U.S. military were coordinating the search mission, Earhart's friend, aviator Jackie Cochran, took a different approach. A believer in extrasensory perception, Cochran announced a few days after the disappearance that she was receiving mental signals about her friend.

In her memoirs, *The Stars at Noon*, Cochran detailed her vision that Earhart had ditched the plane in the ocean, Noonan had fractured his skull, the plane was floating in the open sea, and the two were alive. She urged Putnam to send ships and planes as quickly as possible. Putnam apparently took this suggestion seriously and used it in his efforts to extend the search. Referring to his wife as a "castaway" and to Cochran's belief as having a "strange nature," he cabled the secretaries of commerce and the navy:

FOR YOUR CONFIDENTIAL INFORMATION EXTRAORDI-
NARY EVIDENCE SEEMS TO EXIST INDICATING CAST-
AWAY STILL LIVING THOUGH OF SUCH STRANGE
NATURE CANNOT BE OFFICIAL OR PUBLICLY CON-
FIRMED.

Putnam was also being subjected to dozens of other suggestions—crank calls, letters from people who claimed to have information, and strange hoaxes. Some cases of mistaken information
were well intentioned. For instance, one evening a popular national radio show, "The March of Time," dramatized Earhart's contact with the *Itasca*. Thinking they were hearing the actual voice of
Earhart, listeners flooded police, Coast Guard, and navy phone
lines nationwide to report having heard from the downed flier.

Other reports came from radio hobbyists. Among these were
two amateur radio operators in Los Angeles who claimed they
heard, several days after Earhart's disappearance, weak signals
identifying her call letters, KHAQQ, on 6210 kilocycles. But the
Coast Guard headquarters at San Francisco, which had three radio
stations constantly monitoring, heard nothing despite unusually
good conditions for reception.

Nor was anything heard by the station in Pearl Harbor or in the
radio rooms aboard the *Itasca* or the *Swan*, which was stationed
between Howland and Hawaii. Commander Thompson later testified that what the Los Angeles amateurs heard were, in his opinion, signals from the *Itasca* trying to contact Earhart. He based his
testimony on significant coincidences between the times of transmission from the *Itasca* and the times the amateur operators reported hearing the messages.

Finally, Roosevelt, Putnam, and the others involved in the
search had to admit defeat. On July 19, the massive search was
called off. All told, roughly 250,000 square miles of open sea—an
area as big as Texas—had been searched in a two week period.
When the search ships returned to their home ports, their flags
flew at half-mast. Earhart and Noonan were officially listed as "lost
at sea." The public joined in mourning America's lost heroes.

And the mystery was just beginning.

3 *The Rumors Begin*

It has already been five days since the Earhart plane was first reported missing, and the fate of the missing plane is today generally thought to be pessimistic. Despite this, however, the fact that the United States Navy has set up such an exaggerated search plan raises a suspicion that they may be trying to collect materials for strategic study under the pretense of such an air search.

Japanese consul-general in Honolulu, July 7, 1937,
to Foreign Minister Koki Hirota in Tokyo

Public speculation about the famous fliers began immediately. All around the world, people were wondering: Did they crash into the ocean? Were they floating in the water? Did they sink without a trace? Or were they awaiting rescue on a desert island?

As the days and weeks changed to months and years with no answers, sinister rumors began to surface—rumors about conspiracies, spies, and sabotage. Some people believed that Earhart was actually carrying out a secret mission for the American military against hostile Japanese forces. Her real mission, it was whispered, had been to collect information so sensitive that it could have started a world war.

Dangerous Territory

In 1937, when Earhart disappeared, the winds of war were beginning to blow in the South Pacific. Japan was becoming increasingly aggressive in its occupation of parts of the region. U.S. officials suspected that the Japanese military government was secretly building up its forces in islands it had occupied since World War I, which included the Marianas, Caroline, and Marshall groups. Such action would have been a serious violation of international law.

As it turned out, the concern was justified. Japan was indeed strengthening its naval and air fleets in the South Pacific. By the time of the December 1941 attack on Pearl Harbor, Hawaii—the incident that triggered America's entry into World War II—the Japanese military presence in the Pacific was massive.

"A Very Definite Feeling"

One rumor about Earhart was fueled by a report in the San Francisco *Chronicle* in April 1943. It was headlined: AMELIA EARHART—COLLEGE HEAD THINKS FLIER IS JAP CAPTIVE.

The article explained that M. L. Brittain, the president of Georgia Technical College, along with the presidents of Northwestern University and the Universities of California and Colorado, had been guests of the navy aboard the ship *Colorado* on a cruise to Hawaii in June and July of 1937. Brittain reported that when the ship arrived in Hawaii a radiogram from President Roosevelt instructed the crew to proceed to Howland Island. Brittain said he was given "a very definite feeling A. E. had some sort of understanding with officials of the government" to be on a mission over the Japanese-controlled islands. This report was never fully followed up, and Brittain was dead by the time researcher Fred Goerner found the article in 1960.

A photo of Howland Island, Earhart's final destination.

Was Earhart captured by the Japanese after flying over sensitive areas in the South Pacific, either accidentally or as part of a spy mission?

Throughout her round-the-world flight, Earhart had been careful to avoid politically sensitive territory. Chief among these regions were the Japanese-controlled areas of the South Pacific, which were strictly off-limits to foreigners. Some of these regions were directly adjacent to areas, such as the British-held Gilbert Islands, that were safe for Earhart to pass over. Earhart had to plan her route carefully.

The atmosphere for non-Japanese intruders to these waters was definitely not friendly. All through the 1930s, reports surfaced about incidents of alleged spying in the South Pacific. One involved Willard Price, a National Geographic staff member, who came close to capture by the Japanese while sailing near Truk, one of the Caroline Islands. U.S. Marine Colonel Earl Ellis, while trying to obtain military information around Truk, was captured and never returned. Reports circulated of two American naval officers who were apparently also captured by the Japanese for spying and presumably executed.

During the official search for Earhart and Noonan, the Japanese navy refused to allow U.S. planes and ships to inspect its territories. Japan's refusal to allow other searchers any access only added to the suspicion that it had something to hide. The Japanese government later stated that it conducted its own search of its territories but found nothing. Even years after the end of the war, senior Japanese officers who had served in the Pacific continued to state that their search found no evidence of the fliers.

The man in charge of the Japanese Naval Affairs Bureau in 1937, Inouye Shigeyoshi, said later that he never saw any evidence of Japanese involvement with Earhart. The research of Japanese historian Masataka Chihaya, who investigated the matter, also indicated that the Japanese search failed to find her. Meanwhile, the man who headed the department within the Japanese navy that was responsible for executions strongly denied that any Americans had been executed in the Pacific before or after Earhart's disappearance.

The Mysterious Woman Flier

No American investigator, either, has ever found any hard evidence that the Japanese captured Earhart and Noonan. Even if the Japanese had detained the famous flier and her navigator, many researchers say, the Japanese military would not have kept the incident a secret. It would have been to Japan's advantage, these researchers argue, to announce the capture of the famous woman pilot as proof of American aggression.

Nonetheless, this rumor of capture is by far the most persistent of all the theories about her. Over the years the rumor grew, becoming increasingly elaborate. After the 1944 Allied invasion of the South Pacific, American forces occupied the area. Hundreds of American servicemen heard variations of the "mysterious flier" story from residents of the islands, and it mushroomed as they repeated it to fellow soldiers. The story was embellished in different ways, but the basic plot remained the same: Two fliers, a white male and a white female, crash landed and were captured in Japanese territory before the war. The woman had short hair and wore trousers like a man. The man's head and leg were injured.

In some versions, the Electra crashed into the sea. Sometimes it came down near this atoll; sometimes near that reef. Sometimes it was completely destroyed; sometimes it sustained only slight damage.

As for the man and woman, they were executed in some stories and jailed in others. According to some versions, Earhart lived in

Escaping from Publicity

The research project that called itself Operation Earhart used Earhart's own writings to further its case that her disappearance was planned. For instance, she once wrote, "Courage is the price that life exacts for granting peace." To George Putnam before their wedding, she wrote, "I may have to keep some place where I can go to be by myself now and then, for I cannot guarantee to endure at all times the confinements of even an attractive cage."

These could be read as expressions of an independent spirit, but Operation Earhart saw them as evidence that she wanted to escape her life. Quoting a magazine story about Earhart, researcher Joe Klaas wrote: "Could Amelia Earhart have become so fed up with 'the extravagant curiosity of the world and the intrusions of the autograph hunters' and with a publicity-minded husband that she agreed to perform espionage for her country in exchange for the permanent peace and privacy of an assumed death?"

Amelia poses for a publicity photo. Did the naturally reclusive Earhart tire of the limelight?

semicaptivity in a hotel. One account had her suffering from amnesia and working as a prostitute for Japanese fishermen. In most of the stories, the man was executed and the woman died of dysentery, an infectious disease, commonly caused by poor sanitation, that results in severe diarrhea. According to one variation, the man, angry over not being fed regularly, was killed after he threw a bowl of soup in a guard's face. According to another, the woman was executed during the Allied invasion.

Little or no evidence exists to support the majority of these stories. Yet with so many accounts surfacing over the years, it seems reasonable to believe that two white fliers, one woman and one man, came down somewhere in Japanese-occupied territory sometime during the 1930s.

Whether those two fliers were Earhart and Noonan is unknown. Possibly they were other people entirely whose true identities are now lost. Another possibility is that over the years islanders may have combined a true story about unknown fliers with the massive publicity that surrounded Earhart. As biographer Mary Love put it:

> That this couple was Amelia Earhart and Fred Noonan is open to serious doubt. The testimony of many islanders . . . may well have been made in the light of rewards offered for information, coupled with a genuine desire to please the interrogator [interviewer].

Those Close to Her

Among Earhart's family, friends, and colleagues, opinion was divided as to her fate. Not one of them seriously believed that she had been a spy, although her mother suspected later that Amelia had been on an assignment of some sort. In 1949, Amy told a newspaper reporter, "Amelia told me many things, but there were some things she couldn't tell me. I am convinced she was on some sort of government mission, probably on verbal orders." Amy's notion of her daughter on a secret mission, however, did not come until she was an elderly woman. She naturally wanted to think the best of her daughter and may have put a patriotic spin on Earhart's flight.

Franklin and Eleanor Roosevelt, meanwhile, steadfastly denied that their friend had been on any sort of government mission. Eleanor told reporters at the time, "Franklin and I loved Amelia too much to send her to her death." Historian Arthur Schlesinger Jr.,

Amelia's mother Amy (left) became convinced that Amelia was on a secret government mission when she disappeared.

an authority on the Roosevelt presidency, has stated, "I know of no evidence connecting Roosevelt and Earhart in espionage."

Paul Mantz and Muriel Morrissey, Earhart's sister, were so concerned about the spy rumors that they both wrote to Eleanor Roosevelt soon after the disappearance. Each received her personal assurance that Earhart had not been on a spy mission. Mantz conducted his own investigation and concluded that she went down in the ocean near Howland Island.

Paul Collins, another friend of Earhart and himself a skilled aviator, felt that even the most experienced pilot could miss a target as small as Howland, especially if (as Earhart would have done) that pilot was flying into a bright sunrise after an exhausting flight. After all, Howland is only two miles long and less than a mile wide, with a maximum elevation of twenty-five feet—and with no other nearby islands to help in navigation.

Clarence "Kelly" Johnson, a Lockheed aeronautical engineer who had worked closely with Earhart just before the last flight, concluded after his own investigation that she simply ran out of gas. Denying a rumor that the plane had been outfitted with

Sisters Muriel and Amelia as children. Muriel sought reassurance from Eleanor Roosevelt that Amelia had not been on a spy mission.

cameras, he stated, "The only camera she had was a Brownie [for taking personal snapshots]." Both Collins and Johnson agreed with Mantz that Earhart probably crashed near Howland. So did Carl Allen, the aeronautical reporter who had followed Earhart's career for years.

A well-meaning group called the Amelia Earhart Foundation, which had been formed by Earhart's friends, acquaintances, and colleagues, tried to raise money for a two year search-and-rescue operation. But the foundation was disorganized and ineffective. It finally managed to send a yacht on a month-long search of the Gilbert and Ellice Islands, which had already been inspected by the navy. No significant new evidence was uncovered.

Putnam Persists

Earhart's husband, George Putnam, held on to the possibility that his wife was alive for many years. He continued to explore every lead. Months after the official search was called off, he was still in Washington, D.C., badgering officials to continue looking. Although his funds were limited, he paid for search efforts with the help of various public and private organizations.

He was also besieged with hundreds of letters from people claiming to have evidence of Earhart's whereabouts. He then had to sort through these letters to separate the genuine clues from the nonsense.

For instance, a piece of wood with a message allegedly written by Earhart washed ashore in Alaska, but it proved to be phony. A life raft similar to Earhart's turned up on the coast of Hawaii, but it was a false alarm. A New York janitor arrived one day at Putnam's office with a scarf that he claimed belonged to Earhart and was evidence that she was alive. When the janitor tried to force money from Putnam, authorities investigated and found a fraud. The scarf really was Earhart's, but it had blown into the man's hand by

Used by the Government?

Privately, George Palmer Putnam maintained for the rest of his life a belief that his wife had not been a spy but that the U.S. military had used her disappearance as an excuse to conduct a search of the Pacific and spy on Japan. Quoted in Mary Love's biography of Earhart, Palmer said the naval aircraft carrier *Lexington* "left San Diego amazingly soon after the 'down' message [that Earhart was missing], which led to the logical guess that the planes [aboard the *Lexington*] were loaded with cameras rather than rubber boats, and the motives were practical rather than humanitarian—especially since the *Lexington* couldn't possibly reach the site until days after A. E. and Noonan were certainly dead."

chance years before when he had been in a crowd watching her at a New York airstrip.

Biographer Mary Love points to Putnam's dogged work in following these leads as evidence of his lasting affection for Earhart: "George's touching obsession with continuing the search is a powerful argument about his emotional nature and his love for Amelia." At the same time, Putnam was trying to keep her memory alive in the public eye, out of love and respect for her but also because he needed money. For instance, he used the journal entries and letters she sent him while on the trip—some of which arrived, eerily enough, after her disappearance—to put together another book, *Last Flight*.

Eventually, however, even Putnam concluded that Earhart was gone for good. In part, his reasons were practical. Earhart had to be officially declared dead so that Putnam could file her will. She had never been very rich, and many bills had to be settled. The amount of money left over was small. Putnam even had to sell their beloved house in Rye, New York, to stay ahead of his creditors.

Earhart lands in Honolulu, Hawaii. Husband George Putnam searched for evidence of Earhart's fate long after other efforts had been abandoned.

George and Amelia

In this passage from her book *The Sound of Wings*, biographer Mary Love reflects on the Earhart-Putnam team and what might have happened to Earhart if she had not linked her destiny with Putnam:

"What George did for Amelia's career was threefold. Firstly, he inspired and encouraged her; secondly, he worked on her behalf to publicize her name and reputation, creating openings for a financially viable career in aviation; thirdly, he introduced her to a wide circle of powerful people and obtained the necessary financial backing for her record attempts. Arguably, without this help, Amelia would never have made that final flight with its tragic outcome (for the sponsorship would not have been available to support the venture except to someone of public stature beyond the ordinary); and so Amelia might have lived to a ripe old age."

On January 5, 1939, Amelia Earhart was officially declared dead. The presiding judge, superior court judge Elliot Craig stated, "With all the evidence before me, I can reach no other decision. Amelia Earhart Putnam died on or about July 2, 1937." Normally, survivors must wait seven years before a missing person can be declared dead. Because of Putnam's prestige, fame, and influence with government authorities, he was able to shorten this period to about a year and a half.

Putnam Moves On

During the waiting period, Putnam fell in love with another woman. He married her after Earhart's death became official. When World War II broke out in 1941, Putnam enlisted in the air force, reaching the rank of major. While stationed in the South Pacific, his superiors allowed him to continue his search for Earhart periodically.

One lead he followed concerned an especially bizarre rumor about Earhart—that while captured by the Japanese, she was being forced to perform as Tokyo Rose. Tokyo Rose was the name given to a seductive female disc jockey who frequently broadcasted propaganda to American soldiers in the Pacific. Interspersing her

Flight to a Desert Island?

Biographer Doris Rich has suggested that Earhart was tired of the public limelight and perhaps tired of her high-profile marriage as well. According to an interview with writer Gore Vidal, Earhart confided these feelings to her longtime friend and colleague, Vidal's father Gene Vidal. In *Amelia Earhart*, Rich writes: "Gene told his son [just before the last flight] that Amelia disliked her husband and that she was tired of the constant attention resulting from his publicity of her career. By 1936 she had made up her mind to find a figurative, if not a literal, desert island on which to live."

messages with popular American music, Rose would urge the American troops to give up, reminding them of everything they were missing at home and telling them that their cause was hopeless.

Putnam listened to several of Tokyo Rose's broadcasts while in the Pacific and was firmly convinced that the voice was not Earhart's. After the war, a Japanese-American woman was tried and convicted of treason in San Francisco for having been Tokyo Rose. Some evidence indicates that Tokyo Rose was actually several different women. There is no hard evidence, however, that Earhart was ever one of them.

Eventually, Putnam came to the sad conclusion that his wife had simply crashed into the ocean and died on impact or shortly after.

He also continued to strongly deny that she had been on any sort of secret mission. If he did have any evidence of spying, it seems unlikely that Putnam, the master of publicity, would have missed an opportunity to announce Earhart's heroic actions for her country. His friend and writing colleague Cap Palmer summed up Putnam's attitude when he remarked, "It may be that A. E. served her country wonderfully well . . . but there was never the faintest doubt in G. P.'s mind that A. E. died within a few miles of Howland and the *Itasca*."

Still, the rumors—and the investigations—continued.

 4 *How Did Earhart Die?*

Not much more than a month ago I was on the other shore of the Pacific, looking westward. This evening, I look eastward over the Pacific. In those fast-moving days which have intervened, the whole width of the world has passed behind us except this broad ocean. I shall be glad when we have the hazards of its navigation behind us.

the last words in Amelia Earhart's diary

Hundreds of stories circulated in the South Pacific in the years after Earhart's disappearance. Most of them concerned two white pilots, a woman and a man. As the stories grew and were embellished, they kept the mystery alive. Dozens of researchers, most of them amateur sleuths, began their quest to find out just what happened to Amelia Earhart.

Josephine Blanco Akiyama

One of the most closely examined of these stories was told by Josephine Blanco Akiyama, a native of Saipan in the Northern Marianas Islands. Akiyama's testimony was first detailed in *Daughter of the Sky*, a 1960 book by Captain Paul L. Briand Jr., an assistant professor of English at the U.S. Air Force Academy. In the years since, other researchers, such as CBS radio news reporter Fred Goerner, have also used Akiyama's story as a starting point.

According to the Briand book, Josephine Blanco was eleven years old in the summer of 1937 when an extraordinary thing happened. While taking lunch to her brother-in-law, who worked for the Japanese at a secret seaplane base at Tanapag Harbor on Saipan, she heard a large, two-motored airplane flying overhead. She then watched it come in low and make a crash landing in the harbor.

Josephine joined the workers at the military installation, who were gathered around two white persons who had come from the plane. At first she thought both of them were men, but someone said one was a woman. She was told they were American fliers. As she recalled, "They were both thin and looked very tired. The woman had short-cut hair like a man and she was dressed like a man. The man, I think I remember, had his head hurt in some way." Some soldiers led them away to a clearing in the woods, shots rang out, and the soldiers returned alone.

After the end of the war in 1945, American military forces occupied Saipan. During this period, Josephine Blanco, by then a young woman, worked as an assistant to a U.S. Navy dentist, Dr. Casimir Sheft. She later married another Saipan resident, Maximo Akiyama, and in 1957 they moved to San Mateo, California.

Not until then did she come forward with her remarkable story. Akiyama told Briand that she had once mentioned the incident to her boss, the navy dentist. However, it was not until she moved to America and saw photos of Earhart and Noonan that she realized the people she had seen might really have been the famous fliers. At that point, she decided to make her story public.

What Seems Most Likely

In her book *The Sound of Wings*, Earhart biographer Mary Love generally avoids speculation about Earhart's fate. She does, however, offer this possible story: "The most likely scenario is that the plane was in the vicinity of Howland and may, at one point, have even been within visual distance but missed it either due to clouds in the line of sight (a relatively small cloud would obscure such a small target) or, if the fliers ever emerged into the clear air north of Howland, possibly missed the tiny island in the glare of the rising sun on the water. This, according to eyewitnesses, reduced visibility to a practical fifteen miles or less, although the *Itasca* at that time was making heavy black smoke, which at one point stretched for ten miles.

"What seems most likely is that Amelia ran out of fuel and was forced to land at sea shortly after her last verified message to *Itasca* at 20:14 hours (GMT). . . . All the documented facts point to a ditching off Howland Island, which neither flier survived."

A view of Saipan, where Josephine Blanco Akiyama claimed to have seen Earhart land and be shot by Japanese soldiers.

Fred Goerner tracked down Dr. Sheft, the navy dentist, while researching his 1966 best-seller, *The Search for Amelia Earhart*. Sheft verified Akiyama's story in an interview with Goerner. He confirmed that Josephine Blanco had been his assistant in 1945 and 1946. One day, he recalled, he had been talking with a patient about Earhart.

Sheft recalled, "At that point, Josephine came into the conversation and told us about having seen two American fliers, a man and a woman, on Saipan before the war." Sheft said that he repeated the story to his officers, but no one seemed interested. He added that he thought Akiyama was telling the truth. "After all," he said, "she couldn't have had any reason for inventing such a story back in 1945."

More Tales from Saipan

Goerner made several trips to Saipan in the early 1960s on the trail of Earhart. He interviewed many Saipanese, including Akiyama's brother-in-law, whose recollections usually agreed with Akiyama's story and supported the widespread rumors that Earhart had been imprisoned on the island. One person he interviewed was Matilde San Nicolas, who said that as a young girl on Saipan she had met the white woman the Japanese referred to as "flier and spy." "She was tall and thin and she had not much hair for a woman; it was

61

A Simple Answer

In this brief passage from her book *Amelia Earhart*, biographer Doris Rich sums up the general attitude of Earhart's friends, family, and admirers as to her fate: "Her family, friends, colleagues, and reputable historians all offer the same simple answer. She lost her way on a flight from Lae, New Guinea to Howland Island and died somewhere in the Pacific."

Earhart with Wiley Post and Roscoe Turner, two respected pilots. Both pilots believed what many others believed of Earhart's disappearance—that she had attempted a flight that was too much for her.

short." When Goerner showed San Nicolas pictures of fifteen different women, the woman picked out Earhart without hesitation.

The woman flier, San Nicolas said, had been held captive for months. On occasion she was let out for exercise, and Matilde gave her fruit. One time, the woman took Matilde's geography textbook and wrote something on a map of the Pacific. But Matilde neither spoke nor read English, so she could not understand it. Another time, around 1937 as best Matilde could remember, she saw the woman again, looking ill. She gave Matilde a ring from her finger. The next day, Matilde heard that the woman had died of dysentery.

The geography book was later lost in the 1944 invasion; the ring was passed to a series of Matilde's relatives and also lost.

Goerner also interviewed José Pangelinan, a Saipanese grocer, who related that before the war he had seen an American man and woman who were being held captive. The man had been held in a military police stockade, the woman in a *ryokan* (a Japanese-style rural inn). Pangelinan said that the man was executed the day after the woman's death from disease sometime in the late 1930s, and that they had been buried together in an unmarked grave outside the walls of an old cemetery. He had not witnessed this himself, but had spoken with the officers in charge.

It puzzled Goerner that none of the two hundred people he interviewed had ever come forward with stories like those of Akiyama and Pangelinan. In the opinion of a Catholic priest who was living on Saipan and serving as Goerner's interpreter, the reason was fear. Saipan had been occupied for hundreds of years, and

The prison in Saipan where Amelia Earhart was rumored to have been held by the Japanese.

its natives had been mistreated by many foreign nations, including Spain, Germany, Japan, and America.

According to the priest, the Saipanese had long since learned not to inquire too deeply into sensitive matters. "After such experiences," the priest said, "you can't wonder why most of the Saipanese are not willing to become involved in something that is not really their business."

False Leads

The more he researched, the more Goerner believed he was onto a strong story. However, several promising leads turned into dead ends. He hired divers to search the floor of Tanapag Harbor for evidence of the plane Akiyama reported seeing. They found an airplane generator that appeared to be American. However, technicians from the Bendix Corporation, which had manufactured Earhart's generator, concluded that it was not an American unit. It had probably been built by the Japanese, who made nearly exact copies of American engines for their seaplanes during the 1930s.

Goerner also searched for the grave Pangelinan had described. He found an unmarked burial spot with two skeletons laid head to foot. Excitement grew when a local dentist examined the teeth and said the corpses were probably not Japanese or Saipanese.

Goerner arranged to have the bones brought to San Francisco for inspection by Dr. Theodore McCown, a forensic anthropologist—that is, an expert trained to reconstruct events from bones and other evidence. McCown concluded that the teeth in the grave belonged to at least four people, not one of them Caucasian. He wrote in his report, "The . . . hypothesis that the remains are those of a white American male and female buried not more than twenty-five years ago in the Saipan location, is not supported." A disappointed Goerner arranged for the return of the anonymous remains to Saipan for burial in an official graveyard.

The publicity surrounding the analysis of the bones led Goerner to several other promising stories. One of the many people who contacted Goerner was John Mahan, who served in the navy in the Marshall Islands after the invasion. Mahan said he had heard from a native interpreter, Elieu Jibambam, that two white fliers had crash-landed in 1937 in the ocean between three of the Marshall Islands: Majuro, Jaluit, and Ailinglapalap. Jibambam, who strongly

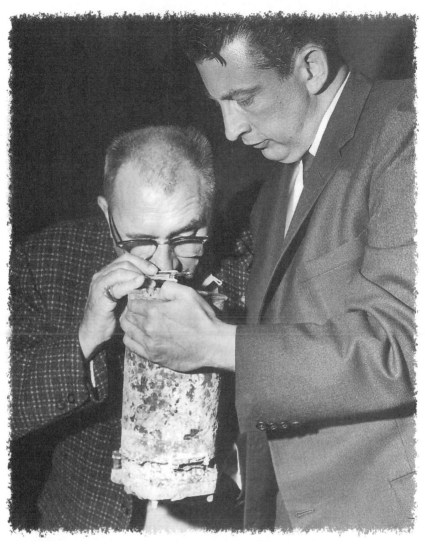

Paul Mantz examines an airplane generator found in the waters off Saipan by Fred Goerner (right). Mantz attempted to identify whether the generator could have come from Earhart's plane.

believed the fliers were Earhart and Noonan, added that they had been picked up by a Japanese fishing boat and taken elsewhere.

The man who had been Mahan's senior officer, Lieutenant Eugene Bogan, confirmed Mahan's story. Bogan told Goerner that he had not been allowed to file a report on the matter because it was only a rumor and might have raised false hopes. He added that in his opinion Jibambam was to be trusted; he was honest and intelligent and would not have made up the story or repeated false information.

A box containing the remains of two human bodies found in Saipan and thought to be those of Earhart and Noonan. The remains were studied in 1961.

Goerner pieced all his information together to devise a theory that Earhart, unable to find Howland Island, had backtracked in search of the Gilbert Islands. She was too far north, however, and crash-landed instead on Mili Atoll in the Marshalls. Around July 13 a Japanese fishing boat picked up the fliers and transferred them to a military ship bound for Saipan.

The plane Josephine Akiyama saw, Goerner argued, was a Japanese plane that took them from the military ship to Tanapag Harbor. The fliers were then held captive on Saipan—Earhart in a private inn called Kobayashi Royokan and Noonan in a jail. He wrote, "Probably there was more than one woman among the prisoners on Saipan, but descriptions of the white woman held at Kobayashi Royokan almost perfectly fitted Earhart." In Goerner's opinion, the fliers died on Saipan—she of dysentery, he by execution—and are buried there still.

More Stories from the Marshalls

Another researcher, retired air force officer Victor Loomis, also concluded that Earhart crash-landed in the Marshalls. While stationed in the Marshalls in 1952, Loomis found the remains of an airplane on a tiny atoll, covered over with coral and vegetation. Years later, wondering if perhaps the plane he had seen was the famous Electra, he began his own investigation.

In his 1985 book, *Amelia Earhart: The Final Story*, Loomis describes how he asked Paul Rafford Jr., a former aviation radio operator and communications expert, to run a computer analysis of the *Itasca*'s radio logs. Rafford's tests indicated that Earhart had been about 150 miles north-northwest of Howland when she sent her last message. Loomis came to the same conclusion as Goerner; he suggested that, after broadcasting this last message, Earhart failed to find Howland, turned back to find the Gilbert Islands, and found the Marshalls instead.

"Somewhere Below Her Ear"

Researcher Victor Loomis interviewed a number of Marshallese residents who confirmed his theory that Earhart crashed there. One was Bilimon Amaran, who had been a medical assistant for the Japanese navy before and during the war. Amaran claimed that in 1937 he was taken aboard the Japanese ship *Kamoi* to treat a white man with wounds on his head and leg. With him was an uninjured white woman wearing trousers, a shirt, and scarf.

The people may have been Fred Noonan and Amelia Earhart, but Amaran's testimony was imprecise and inconclusive. For instance, at one point in his interview, Amaran said the woman's hair was "somewhere below her ear." Loomis prompted, "The lady we're talking about was slender, and her hair was fairly short for the time." Amaran replied, "Yes, her hair was light . . . light color, sure. And her hair, that's why I say that, her hair was somewhere around about the level of her ear."

Amaran said that the Japanese naval officers told him the pair had been picked up on a reef near Mili Atoll, off Majuro Island. Amaran also told Loomis that after he treated the man, the pair's airplane was hauled on board the *Kamoi* with a canvas sling. Both strangers and the plane were taken away. Amaran thought they may have gone to Saipan.

Loomis collected numerous stories that seemed to support his theory that Earhart crashed in the Marshalls. One Marshallese man testified that he had witnessed an airplane, which he thought was Earhart's, crash on Mili Atoll. Still another reported that he saw a white woman and man paddle ashore from that same crash and bury a mysterious silver container in the sand. Finally, Tony de Brum, a well-respected local politician, told Loomis:

> We all know about this woman who was reported to have come down on Mili . . . , was captured by the Japanese and taken off to Jaluit. I believe this is exactly what happened. Remember, the stories were being told long before you Americans began asking questions.

Loomis's final conclusion was similar to Goerner's. Loomis suggested that after crashing in the Marshalls, the fliers were held cap-

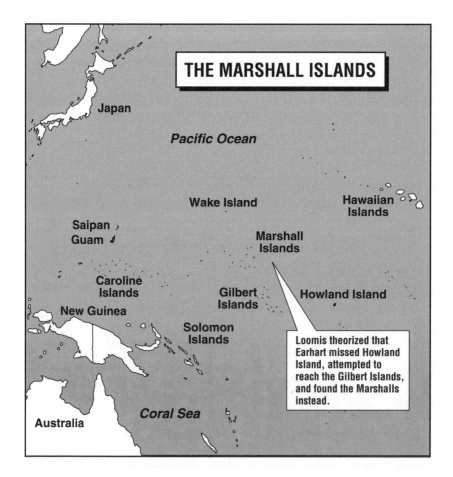

THE MARSHALL ISLANDS

Japan

Pacific Ocean

Wake Island

Hawaiian Islands

Saipan
Guam

Marshall Islands

Caroline Islands

Gilbert Islands

Howland Island

New Guinea

Solomon Islands

Loomis theorized that Earhart missed Howland Island, attempted to reach the Gilbert Islands, and found the Marshalls instead.

Coral Sea

Australia

tive on Saipan; while imprisoned, Earhart died of dysentery and Noonan was executed. He also concluded that, in his opinion, the fliers were "the first prisoners of war and casualties in a conflict yet to come."

Earhart's Blindfold?

Evidence suggesting that Earhart did not die of disease, but was instead executed by the Japanese, was uncovered by still another investigator. T. C. "Buddy" Brennan, a Texas businessman, became interested in Earhart while scouring the South Pacific for salvageable World War II–era Japanese planes. In his 1988 book, *Witness to the Execution: The Odyssey of Amelia Earhart*, Brennan wrote about his research.

He interviewed a number of people who claimed to have seen Earhart on Saipan after her disappearance. The most intriguing testimony came from Nieves Cabrera Blas. As a young woman on Saipan, Blas claimed, she saw Earhart being executed.

Blas told Brennan that a woman pilot, whom Blas thought was Earhart, had been held captive on Saipan all through the war. Blas said that during the American invasion of the island she saw three Japanese motorcycles speed by her. In a sidecar, handcuffed and blindfolded, was the woman pilot.

Blas followed the motorcycles, then hid and watched as the soldiers took her to an isolated area. She told Brennan:

> I watch and they take her to this place where there is a hole been dug. They make her kneel in front when they tear the blindfold from her face and throw it in the hole. The soldiers shoot her in the chest and she fall backwards into the grave. I run from that place so the soldiers do not see me. Later, I go back to see if they bury her, and they had.

Blas led Brennan to what she said was the place of execution. It had since become a storage area for heavy road-building equipment. On a second trip to Saipan, Brennan got permission to dig in this area with a bulldozer. He uncovered a scrap of cloth that at first puzzled him, but which he later realized could have been the blindfold Blas had described. He wrote:

> Stained black and somewhat tattered, it had a definite shape but not one I could immediately identify. . . . It had

T. C. "Buddy" Brennan holds the tattered cloth he believes to be the blindfold Earhart wore minutes before she was executed in 1944 by the Japanese.

been cut to a distinct pattern: portions of a stitched hem were faintly discernable. . . . The cloth is made of cotton fiber, consistent with fabrics in general use during the early '40s. There is nothing to indicate it was woven more recently than 50 years ago.

Another researcher, Thomas Devine, also concluded that Earhart had been executed on Saipan. He based his conclusion, in part, on a *Japan Times* interview from November 1970, which he details in his 1987 book, *Eyewitness: The Amelia Earhart Incident*. In the interview, a woman named Michiko Sugita stated that her father, Mikio Suzuki, had been the civilian chief of police at Garapan, the village on Saipan that is often mentioned in stories about Earhart's capture.

Sugita was eleven in 1937, she said, when she overheard policemen describe to her father the execution of an American woman aviator. Some officials had argued at the time that the woman did not deserve death, but Mikio Suzuki disagreed. His daughter remembered him saying, "Since she came here to carry on her duties as a spy, it cannot be helped that she be executed."

Is the Plane Still Intact?

Randall Brink, a pilot and aviation editor who studied the Earhart case, believed that Earhart was shot down over the Marshalls and captured by the Japanese. But he also speculated in his 1994 book, *Lost Star: The Search for Amelia Earhart*, that she was taken to Tokyo for execution—and that her airplane may still be intact somewhere.

Brink's opinion was that Earhart was shot down over the Marshalls, probably by a Japanese plane from the carrier *Akagi*. After analyzing her last radio signals, he concluded that she was about three hundred miles northwest of Howland, and thus over the Marshalls, at the time of the last message. He wrote:

> [W]e know that the Japanese were there in considerable force, waiting, listening, monitoring the radio transmissions and the progress of the flight. It is no exaggeration to say that Amelia flew into the midst of a major Japanese naval exercise then under way in the southeastern Marshalls, made up of at least three destroyers, one battleship, one seaplane tender, and the supercarrier *Akagi*.

He also agreed that the fliers were captured and taken to the headquarters of the Japanese Pacific Central Command on Saipan.

The evidence Brink offered to support his theory was an interview with two Marshallese brothers, John and Dwight Heine. The Heine brothers worked for the Japanese at the naval aviation docks at Taroa, on the northern part of Maloelap Atoll. They stated that in 1937 they helped unload from a ship an airplane that was missing one wing. The plane's passengers, a Caucasian woman and man, stayed aboard the ship.

According to the brothers, the plane was stored with others on shore and later moved to a hangar inland. Since surface buildings in Taroa were not badly damaged during the Allied invasion, Brink suggested that these hangars might still be intact. "Sitting in one of them, in all probability . . . is the fuselage of a Lockheed Electra, perhaps still containing the sixty-five hundred first-day-of-issue philatelic covers, now with an estimated value of over $25 million."

Brink's research indicated that Earhart was alive until at least the end of 1937. His evidence was the testimony of an American Jesuit priest who was in the South Pacific at the time. The priest, who was fluent in Japanese, overheard a conversation in late 1937 between two Japanese military officers. The officers were talking about an American woman pilot who had been captured and brought to Tokyo to stand trial. Brink speculated that Earhart may have been secretly tried, found guilty, and executed in Tokyo.

The Smuggled Nun

One of the most bizarre of all the Earhart theories came out of research done in the 1960s by a retired air force major, Joseph Gervais. Helped by two other Earhart buffs and former military men, Robert Dinger and Joe Klaas, Gervais conducted an investigation called Operation Earhart.

One of the many complex conclusions put forth in Klaas's 1970 book about the project, *Amelia Earhart Lives*, was that Earhart did not die in the South Pacific or in Tokyo. According to Klaas, she was taken prisoner by the Japanese and held at the Imperial Palace in Tokyo until the end of the war. She left Tokyo disguised

Joseph Gervais (left) and Joe Klaas hold pieces of wreckage that they believe came from Earhart's plane during her ill-fated flight. The men believe that Earhart survived eight years of Japanese captivity.

as a nun and secretly reentered the United States. As of 1970, she was living under a false name in New Jersey. This arrangement was necessary, according to Klaas, because of a complex political deal that had been arranged between America and Japan after the war. Earhart was released by the Japanese in exchange for a guarantee that the Japanese emperor, Hirohito, would not be tried as a war criminal.

Smuggling Earhart

Gervais suggested that at the end of the war, Jackie Cochran smuggled Earhart out of Tokyo disguised as one of five Roman Catholic nuns who had been prisoners of war there. It is apparently true that, following their release, five unidentified nuns accompanied Cochran on a flight to China. Cochran wrote about this episode in her autobiography, *The Stars at Noon,* but she did not identify the nuns individually.

The Operation Earhart team based its theory that Earhart was one of the nuns on a portion of Cochran's book. In this section, Cochran describes wartime meetings in China and the Philippines with Francis Cardinal Spellman, then an archbishop of the Catholic Church and chief chaplain of the U.S. military forces. Apparently, Gervais and his colleagues felt that a series of meetings with a Catholic head chaplain of the military might logically conclude with the use later of a nun's habit as a disguise. As Klaas wrote:

> [T]he problem of how to get anyone as easily recognizable and as big news as Amelia Earhart past the curious eyes of aircraft crews and reporters might have been solved by evacuating her in the concealing garments of a Catholic nun.

Gervais's second startling allegation—that Earhart was living under an assumed name in New Jersey—was inspired by a chance meeting. In 1965 he spoke to a group of pioneer fliers and their families at a gathering on Long Island. At the luncheon afterwards, he met a New Jersey woman, Irene Bolam, who, he said, resembled what Amelia Earhart would look like if she were alive in 1965.

According to Klaas, a chill ran through Gervais when he laid eyes on Bolam. Klaas quoted him as saying:

> I don't know if I can describe what happened to me. For five years I had been living with this Earhart thing. I had

Irene Bolam, holding a copy of Amelia Earhart Lives, *tells reporters that she is not Amelia Earhart. The author of the book, Joe Klaas, refuses to believe her denials.*

been reading about Earhart, asking about Earhart, speculating about Earhart, studying photographs of Earhart . . . and then, all of a sudden, right there across a room in the Sea Spray Inn, I thought I recognized her.

The similarities, Gervais thought, were more than just physical. Bolam was wearing a military major's oak-leaf decoration and a miniature ribbon signifying the Distinguished Flying Cross. Earhart had been an honorary major in the Army Air Corps, and she had been awarded the Cross after her transatlantic solo flight. Bolam told Gervais, moreover, that she belonged to the Ninety-Nines, an organization of pioneer women fliers, and to Zonta, a women's service organization. Earhart had belonged to both. When Gervais asked her about Earhart, Bolam replied calmly that she had known Earhart well and had, in fact, flown with her on occasion.

Searching for Amelia

Despite evidence and testimony from people such as pioneer pilot Viola Gentry, who had known both Bolam and Earhart in the 1920s, Gervais insisted that no identifying records, such as a pilot's license, existed for Irene Bolam before 1937. According to him, Irene Craigmile (as she was known before her several marriages) did not receive a pilot's license until June 1, 1937—the day Earhart took off from Miami on her final flight. As Klaas put it, "Did Irene Craigmile, alias Irene O'Crowley, alias Irene Heller, alias Mrs. Guy Bolam, begin to exist only as Amelia Earhart soared on wings of mystery across the horizon?" Other researchers argue that the 1937 license was simply a renewal, and the identical date a coincidence.

When Gervais tried to interview Irene Bolam, she refused: "Look, Major Gervais, I once had a public life," she told him. "I once had a career in flying. But I've retired. I've given all that up now." When Gervais insisted, she made a date to meet him in the lobby of a hotel in Montreal, Canada, but never showed up.

When he tried to contact her later, Gervais said, her nurse would not let her come to the phone. Guy Bolam offered to fly with Gervais to North Carolina, where the Bolams had another home. Gervais said Guy Bolam did not show up for the flight, and when the investigator went to North Carolina alone, Mrs. Bolam again refused to talk with him.

To the press, Irene Bolam strongly denied any connection with Amelia Earhart apart from their previous friendship. When Klaas's book came out, she successfully sued his publishing company for libel. The book was withdrawn from general circulation, though it can still be found in some public libraries. Irene Bolam died in 1982.

There has been much speculation on how, when, and under what circumstances Amelia Earhart died. In addition, at least as much energy and thought has been put to the question of why she was in the South Pacific in the summer of 1937. Although no hard evidence exists to support the theory, and despite repeated government denials, many researchers believe that Amelia Earhart was carrying out an espionage mission for the United States when she disappeared.

CHAPTER 5
Was Earhart a Spy?

Some theories rely on outright sensationalism, others on detailed detective work based on a snippet of information that caught the attention of the researcher. In some, one can see the author almost unconsciously manipulating what is known to match and prove a theory.

Mary Love, *The Sound of Wings*

The most persistent of all the rumors about Amelia Earhart was that she was a spy for the American government. If she was not a genuine, full-time spy, the theory goes, at least she had been asked by the government to carry out a secret mission while flying over the South Pacific.

According to this theory, Earhart's round-the-world voyage was little more than a cover story that allowed her to make a secret surveillance trip over Japanese-held territory. Adding fuel to this idea was the fact that back in 1929 Earhart had been named an honorary major in the 381st Army Air Corps Reserve. Many people believe that this honorary title was evidence of Earhart's connection to military operations in the Pacific.

Flight for Freedom

The public discussion began in 1942, when George Putnam's friend Cap Palmer published an article in *Skyways* magazine called "The War's First Casualty?" It detailed the various Earhart-as-spy rumors that had surfaced. The rumors were intensified after the release of a very popular 1943 movie, *Flight for Freedom*. This film was clearly based on Earhart, and it was advertised as "The Story They Couldn't Tell Before Pearl Harbor." Thousands of Americans at home as well as thousands more still serving in the South Pacific, saw the film.

A Deep Canyon

Many individuals and privately funded groups have gone to the South Pacific in search of Earhart. One such group based in Cleveland, Ohio, made two brief expeditions there in 1967 and 1968. Team leader Donald Kothera had seen a twin-engine plane in a deep canyon while stationed on Saipan in 1946. He suspected it was Earhart's, and the team he assembled wanted to find it again. Unfortunately, all they found were a few parts of the aircraft, which they determined had been produced sometime before 1937. They also found some burned bones, which they claimed were the remains of a female, probably white and between forty and forty-two years old.

In the movie, Rosalind Russell plays a famous American flier, Tonie Carter, who is asked by her government to fly over the South Pacific just before the outbreak of war. Carter is to deliberately ditch her plane and go into hiding on a remote island. The navy, using a search for her as an excuse, can thus spy on Japanese installations. But when the plan is discovered by the Japanese, Carter deliberately crashes into the ocean rather than risk capture.

In the movie's subplot, Carter's navigator, played by Fred Mac-Murray, is also her old boyfriend. Since the public assumed that *Flight for Freedom* was a more-or-less true version of the Earhart story, this twist gave rise to still another widespread rumor: that Earhart and Noonan had engineered their disappearance so that they could live together in isolation. Many people eagerly latched on to this idea. As one letter to the editor of the New York *Daily News* put it, "If they are not found I will always think of them as Queen Amelia and King Frederick of some island."

Earhart's husband, George Putnam, was so offended by the rumors of a love affair between Earhart and Noonan that he successfully sued the movie's producers, RKO Studios, and settled out of court for twenty-five hundred dollars—a substantial sum in the early 1940s.

New Engines?

One researcher who believed the Earhart-as-spy theory was Fred Goerner, the man who thought he had once found Earhart's grave.

Fred Goerner holds a piece of wreckage in Garapan Harbor in a second expedition to retrieve wreckage. This expedition proved that the plane in the harbor was not Earhart's.

His conclusions were based partly on his analysis of State Department and navy files.

Among these files were documents indicating that Earhart's flight had been delayed in Australia, officially because of "health certificates" and evidence that the radio equipment had been checked and repaired there. Most intriguing, however, was some odd, sketchy evidence that could be interpreted to mean that new, more powerful engines had also been installed in Earhart's plane in Australia.

Goerner said that this conclusion could be reached only by closely analyzing a large amount of strange and apparently random material in the files. He suggested that someone had, for some reason, deliberately left these documents in the files, assuming that researchers at a later date would eventually put together the pieces and understand their meaning. According to Goerner, material that to a casual observer seemed to be unconnected to anything else in the file actually revealed the key to the engine replacement.

The new engines would have given the Electra half again as much power as before, with a cruising speed of over two hundred miles per hour. Goerner wrote:

The added power [of the new engines] altered every computation that had been publicly made for the flight. . . . The report that she checked in with Lae, New Guinea, about 800 miles en route to Howland averaging 111 miles per hour had to be phony; either that or the plane was encountering nearly one-hundred-mile-per-hour head winds.

Faced with such headwinds, Goerner stated, Earhart would surely have turned back to Lae. With her new, more powerful engines, however, Earhart was instead able to fly over the Japanese-held island of Truk to observe its airfield and fleet. She used the added power of the new engines to stay on schedule while she went hundreds of miles off course.

Secret Cameras?

Another angle on the Earhart-as-spy story came from Randall Brink in his book *Lost Star.*

One of Brink's conclusions was that the Electra was specifically purchased for Earhart by the U.S. government so that she could carry out espionage. Officially, Purdue University, where Earhart taught, had bought the plane for Earhart to use as a teaching and research tool. Brink argued, however, that Purdue merely acted as a front for the deception. For this and other conclusions he

The Planter and the Bones

Many strange stories turned up as a result of the publicity surrounding Fred Goerner's investigation. One came from a former Coast Guardsman who said that he had served on Gardner Island, one of the Phoenix Islands, during the war. Natives there had told him of the skeleton of a woman and the skull of a man that were found on the shore in late 1938. A white planter on the island thought the remains might be Earhart and Noonan, and he set out in a boat with the bones and some native helpers. But the planter died en route to another island where he hoped to verify his claim, and the superstitious natives threw both the bones and the planter overboard.

A *Chauffeur?*

Researcher Fred Goerner followed many false leads. At one point, someone who had been a corporal with the army engineers during the occupation of Saipan sent Goerner a copy of a photo of Earhart that he had found in the ruins of a home there. It showed her seated on the running board of a black automobile. A man, apparently Asian and wearing an officer's cap, could be seen standing on the other side of the car.

At first, Goerner thought that the photo indicated Earhart had been a captive of the Japanese military. However, Goerner discovered that the photograph had been taken in Honolulu after Earhart's first unsuccessful attempt at the flight. The man in the "officer's cap" was a chauffeur.

A similar incident involved a photograph reproduced in Joe Klaas's book *Amelia Earhart Lives*. The photo shows

Earhart dressed in a Japanese kimono, being served tea. Klaas cited it as evidence of Earhart's capture. However, biographer Mary Love, in her book *The Sound of Wings,* proved that the photo was actually taken in Hawaii prior to Earhart's solo transpacific flight.

Fred Goerner, author of The Search for Amelia Earhart.

reached, he cited his discovery and analysis of various classified military and government documents hidden since the war.

He believed the military gave Earhart further assistance, such as the use of airfields in Hawaii and California, that would not normally have gone to a civilian. He also claimed that the airstrip on Howland Island was built especially for her trip, rather than for the official reason—that it was to be part of a planned South Pacific air route. Brink suggests that Earhart's mission received backing from the president himself. Roosevelt and Earhart were friends; besides, as Brink put it, the military would not give a civilian such extensive help "without orders . . . from the highest possible level."

Furthermore, Brink felt that the testimony of Earhart's secretary, Margot de Carrie, was significant. De Carrie stated that a number of senior military and government officials had visited Earhart's California home while preparations for the flight were under way. According to Brink, de Carrie said that no further bills for repairs, fuel, storage, or anything else connected with the Electra came to Earhart following her meeting with the influential businessman and presidential adviser Bernard Baruch.

Earhart's Flight a Hoax?

Brink concluded that Earhart's entire first attempt to fly around the world was phony. He claimed that Earhart's Electra 10E was secretly exchanged after the crash in Hawaii for a faster, smaller, and lighter Electra 12, which had a greater range and could fly higher than the 10E. This new plane, he said, was also outfitted with spy cameras.

As evidence, Brink cited an interview with Robert T. Elliott, an airframe technician at Lockheed at the time. Elliott pointed out that each Electra, because there were so few of them and the technology was changing so fast, was virtually hand built. In other words, each new model was a unique prototype. Consequently, secret modifications could be made with relative ease. According to Elliott, the same identification number, NR 16020, was painted on the new plane to enhance the deception. Elliott also stated that he was instructed to cut two large holes for cameras in the lower aft [rear] portion of the airplane's fuselage.

Brink saw it as sinister that Earhart did little promotional work during the period between the failed first attempt and her last flight. In his opinion, Earhart and her colleagues did not want to draw

A case of artifacts containing aircraft skin, shoe heels, and other evidence found by Richard Gillespie in 1992. Gillespie believes the evidence proves that Earhart went down with her plane somewhere in the Pacific.

undue publicity to themselves during this crucial period of secret plane switching and modification. Brink wrote, "Maintaining a low profile, she gave few newspaper or radio interviews, in contrast to her usual practice of being in the news on a more or less daily basis."

Brink also analyzed Earhart's last radio messages and concluded that they supported his theory of the switched plane. At about 6:45 on the morning she disappeared, she radioed a message that she was about one hundred miles out. About an hour later, at 7:42, she radioed that she was very close; the signal was clear and strong, which would indicate that she was indeed close.

According to Brink, Earhart could have traveled such a distance only in a plane with engines more powerful than she was supposed to have:

> Obviously, an airplane that actually covers a hundred miles in half an hour has a surface speed of two hundred miles per hour. It was well known that the Electra 10E, the plane Earhart started out with in Hawaii, had an optimum speed

of only 140 miles an hour. In addition, because she was flying into a headwind, her speed over the surface would have been cut to less than that. No one knew, of course, that Earhart was actually flying an aircraft that was perfectly capable of a two-hundred-mile-per-hour speed, even with a headwind.

According to Brink, Earhart left behind her standard radio equipment and the cumbersome trailing antenna because the new Electra was secretly fitted with experimental direction-finding equipment. The new equipment was needed for communication with equipment already aboard the *Itasca*. As Brink put it:

> The reason given publicly was to save weight. Some theorists, unaware of the secret DF [direction-finding] installation, have argued that the removal of the standard equipment made it impossible for Earhart and Noonan to find Howland and may have cost them their lives.

The Itasca, *the ship that kept in contact with Earhart on her last flight. Was Earhart on a secret spying expedition for the U.S. Navy?*

But Brink argued that this standard equipment was simply unnecessary because of the new, top-secret equipment.

As further evidence of Earhart's clandestine activity, Brink cited an interview he did with Walter McMenamy. McMenamy was an amateur Los Angeles radio operator who was part of the informal communications network George Putnam had set up alongside the official navy network. McMenamy said that in the weeks before the first attempt Earhart had written a number of cheerful letters

Earhart with Paul Mantz. Many inconsistencies about the official explanation for Earhart's disappearance leave lingering doubts.

to him. However, when she returned to California after the crash she was rushed off by navy personnel. She recognized McMenamy, he said, with only "a wan smile." Brink added, "Years later, he still remembered his astonishment that she seemed so uncharacteristically subdued and downcast."

Clues

Brink also found evidence of spying once the final flight was under way. He thought it was odd that Earhart's engines were, as she reported in her journals, overhauled in Java, the stop she made before Lae. Although her journals and testimony from many people indicate that she had had problems with the engines all along, Brink said she had not previously complained of engine trouble. The engines were brand-new, well maintained, and not ready for a scheduled overhaul.

If Earhart really had an engine problem, Brink reasoned, she probably would have stopped for repairs at the modern facilities in Singapore, instead of waiting until she landed at the primitive airfield in Java. Brink speculated that the real mission of the mechanics who serviced the Electra at Java was to "check out how accurately the cameras were working, and make any necessary adjustments before the big shoot."

Brink also found fault with the official reason for changing the direction of the flight after the crash in Hawaii. The official excuse concerned changes in the prevailing wind conditions along the equator. According to Brink, however, this reason was nonsensical. Brink argued that seasonal change in wind direction along the equator is minimal. On her new west-to-east itinerary, he said, Earhart would have to battle headwinds all the way, instead of making use of tailwinds.

Aviators generally would rather have tailwinds to speed them up, rather than headwinds to slow them down. But Brink argued that bad news for an aviator made perfect sense for a spy mission over the Marshalls. On the original east-to-west flight, Earhart would have landed at Lae after her flight over Japanese-held islands. She would have had to unload her secret cameras and film in New Guinea—a non-American, unsecured territory. By traveling west to east, however, she could land at tightly controlled, U.S.-held Howland Island, where any evidence of espionage could have been removed easily and quickly from the plane.

Joseph Gervais, head of Operation Earhart, also believed Earhart had been on a secret reconnaissance mission for the U.S. government.

A Spy or Not a Spy

That Earhart was *not* a spy is one of the conclusions reached by Victor Loomis, the former air force officer who wrote *Amelia Earhart: The Final Story*. In Loomis's opinion, Earhart was simply an unfortunate victim of circumstances. He believed that she and Noonan were innocent of spying but had the bad luck to crash in the Marshalls, where they were taken captive and probably executed.

He found no evidence that intelligence-gathering equipment had been installed on her plane. He pointed out that her departure time from Lae put her over the key Japanese-held areas at night, making surveillance useless. Loomis also thought that Earhart's Quaker background, with its strong emphasis on nonviolence, would have kept her from taking an active part in warlike activities.

On the other hand, the Operation Earhart group led by Joseph Gervais concluded that Earhart had been a very conscious and willing spy. Like Brink, this group suspected that the crash in

Hawaii was deliberate. By damaging her first plane she was able to secretly switch the 10E for a different plane while it was "being repaired" in Oakland.

The new plane, Gervais claimed, was not the Electra 12 (as Brink concluded) but the XC35, a military version of the 10E. Outwardly the two planes looked the same, but the XC35 had more powerful engines and an increased range. It could also be pressurized, which would let it reach much higher altitudes than any civilian airplane. Gervais estimated it could travel fifteen hundred miles off the official course, undetected, and still stay on schedule.

Gervais based his theory in part on some fuzzy photographs that he said showed Earhart's plane in Hawaii, surrounded by military personnel. In his opinion, no civilian would rate such a guard unless something very important had been going on.

He also based his conclusion on an interview with an officer, Lieutenant Colonel Joseph Pellegrini. Gervais heard a rumor at a party that Pellegrini had installed secret cameras in the new plane and tracked the colonel down. Pellegrini denied the allegation vehemently when interviewed by Operation Earhart. However, he did say that in 1939 he had drawn up guidelines for using a camera for a woman aviator who was going to search for Earhart in the area around Truk. Pellegrini said he could not remember that pilot's name. According to Gervais, the only woman flier who was even in the South Pacific in the 1930s was Amelia Earhart.

Flight Over Japan

Earhart's true plan, Gervais felt, was essentially the same as the scenario shown in the movie *Flight for Freedom*. That is, she was asked to fly over Japanese territory, including the islands of Truk, Ponape, Kusaiem, and Tarawa, to take pictures. She was instructed to deliberately ditch the plane on Canton Island, one of the islands in the Phoenix Group, so that the U.S. Navy would have an excuse to search Japanese-held areas.

Various theories and rumors about how Earhart died and whether or not she was a spy have been rampant for years. Almost as widespread as these rumors has been another aspect of the mystery—the theory that Earhart's true mission and final fate were (and still are) the subject of a massive cover-up by both the American and Japanese governments.

6 Was There a Government Cover-Up?

[T]he story of what happened to Amelia Earhart and Fred Noonan is at last falling into place, piece by piece. Each new discovery underscores a fundamental, and disturbing, fact: the truth conflicts with the official and traditionally accepted versions.

Randall Brink, *Lost Star*

Public speculation that both the American and Japanese governments have conspired to cover up the facts about Earhart is widespread. On several occasions, it has reached such a high level of interest that both governments have taken the unusual step of officially and publicly denying any knowledge of a cover-up.

Nonetheless, the theory persists that somewhere—hidden away in a secret government vault in Washington or Tokyo or both—a thick file lies waiting. This file, the story goes, will once and for all prove whether Amelia Earhart was or was not a spy. It will not only clarify what happened to her but also explain just how and why Earhart did what she did.

In part, speculation about a cover-up stems from a passage in the autobiography of Earhart's old friend Jackie Cochran in which Cochran describes her adventures in Tokyo immediately following Japan's surrender. The U.S. military had asked Cochran to visit occupied Japan and prepare a report on the role of women in the Japanese air force. While there, she says, she saw a number of files about Earhart in the Dai Ichi Building, one of the main government centers in Tokyo. She did not describe the contents of those files in detail, a fact to which some researchers have attached a sinister meaning.

However, to most serious Earhart biographers this conclusion seems unlikely. Cochran herself believed, based on her own psychic visions, that her friend had drifted in the ocean for several

The Route of the Kamoi

For his 1985 book *Amelia Earhart: The Final Story*, Victor Loomis interviewed a veteran of the Japanese navy who had served aboard the ship *Kamoi*. This man had what he said were the ship's logs, although Loomis did not explain why such important documents were in the sailor's possession. According to the records, at the time of Earhart's disappearance on July 2, the *Kamoi* was stationed in Saipan in the Mariana Islands. It left there on July 4 and arrived in Japan on July 10.

This information directly contradicts official Japanese intelligence reports, which stated that the ship had been searching for Earhart in the Marshall Islands at the time. He wrote: "Clearly the Japanese had lied to the United States. What were they trying to hide, and why had they gone to so much trouble to make the *Kamoi* appear as if it were on a search mission?" Loomis speculated that the *Kamoi* was actually used to transport Earhart and Noonan to Saipan and possibly on to Tokyo, but the official story was that it had conducted an unsuccessful search.

days before dying. If Cochran had seen something in the files that revealed anything contrary to this, she would certainly have commented on it. Most serious Earhart researchers assume, then, that the files contained only a collection of cuttings and photographs taken from the dozens of newspaper articles from around the world that had been appearing about Earhart for years. Cochran did not describe them, they argue, simply because she felt they were not important—or because she could not read any language besides English.

A Saipanese School for Spies?

Fred Goerner, the CBS radio news reporter, believed that the U.S. government was constantly trying to undermine his efforts to learn about the fate of Earhart. For instance, he said that during one of his trips to Saipan, in 1961, the navy (which still had official control of the island) deliberately sent him on useless wild goose chases. He claimed that navy officials even tried to spread rumors among island residents that he was there to somehow do evil.

Fred Goerner examines the box containing what he believes to be the remains of Amelia Earhart. Goerner claimed the navy made several attempts to prevent him from bringing the remains back to the United States for study.

Goerner wrote that he could not understand why the government wanted to block his investigations—unless it had something serious to protect. In his book, he describes one possibility: that he had stumbled unwittingly on evidence of a secret American training ground for counterspies on Saipan. Goerner reasoned that the military could not allow an open investigation of anything on Saipan for fear of breaching the training camp's security. At one point, the navy confiscated all of Goerner's movie film and photographic negatives. When the photos and film were finally returned, several shots taken at the north end of the island—the location of the alleged training camp—were missing.

When Goerner uncovered what he believed was the gravesite of Earhart and Noonan, the navy immediately declared that the bones could not leave Saipan. Eventually, Goerner received permission to fly the bones to San Francisco for analysis. Even then, Goerner claimed, he was harassed at every turn.

Differences in Radio Records

The primary radio log of the *Itasca*, kept by Leo Bellarts, records one of Earhart's last messages as "KHAQQ calling *Itasca*. We must be on you but cannot see you but gas is running low. Been unable to reach you by radio. We are flying at altitude 1,000 feet." But a second log kept by another radioman reads: "Earhart says running out of gas. Only half hour left/can't hear us at all/we hear her and are sending on 3105 and 500 same time constantly and listening for her frequently."

Of the differences between the two logs, biographer Mary Love wrote: "These two accounts have been taken by some researchers as sinister evidence. Why, they have asked, is Amelia sometimes quoted as saying 'gas is running low' and at other times, 'running out of gas, only half an hour left'?

"Reading the pages of these logs, and pages of radio transmissions unrelated to the Earhart mission, the reason is obvious. This mission, while interesting, was really not very special. It was just another job for *Itasca*; she had performed a similar task some months earlier for the Pan Am survey [on possible South Pacific air routes]. The men keeping those logs had no reason to believe that their scribbled 'radio shorthand' notes would be the subject of countless books. Busy with their duties, they recorded the gist of what they heard, rather than the *precise* wording. . . .

"The sensational suggestions by several writers that [a deliberate effort] was done on instructions of the U.S. government to cover up or distort the facts may be discounted if only because of the wealth of information that exists from so many sources, ranging from the military records to the press (not renowned for keeping secrets) and the inhabitants of various islands."

As evidence he cites the fact that before he could organize the shipment, the navy sent the remains to the States with no prior warning. Goerner's story, which he had wanted to keep secret so that he could have a news exclusive, suddenly hit the media. Hundreds of people showed up at the San Francisco airport in the middle of the night to catch a glimpse of the plane bearing the bones. Goerner's scoop was ruined, and he had to scramble to keep things in control. In addition, he said, his attempts to find information about Earhart in government files met with an unending series of obstacles.

Official Denials

The official position of both the U.S. and Japanese governments has always been to deny any evidence that Earhart was engaged in spy activity. In reaction to the publicity surrounding the bones uncovered by Goerner, both governments again officially denied that Earhart had ever been involved in any kind of covert mission. Hitoshi Tsunoda, an official in the War History Department of the Japanese Defense Agency, declared, "It is impossible and nothing more than nonsense to think the fliers wandered far enough off course to land at Saipan." Even if Earhart and Noonan had been picked up elsewhere by a Japanese fishing boat, he added, they would not have been taken to Saipan. Instead, they would have gone to Palau in the southern Marianas, the headquarters of Japan's South Pacific government.

However, basing his conclusions on government files, Goerner decided that the government had implemented a massive cover-up from the very beginning. President Roosevelt knew of Earhart's mission and capture, Goerner claimed, but had been forced to remain silent because the prewar Pacific situation had been so explosive. U.S. forces were still too unprepared for a war that would no doubt have been triggered by a search of Japanese-held territory. To temporarily keep the peace and prepare for the coming war, Goerner said, Roosevelt was forced to sacrifice his friend.

Goerner also speculated that Harry Truman, who succeeded Roosevelt as president, kept silent about the Earhart matter out of respect for Roosevelt's reputation as a leader. After Truman's term, Goerner argued, the truth might have come out. By that time, however, Saipan had become home to the spy school and thus remained off-limits to reporters. Also, Goerner felt, the nature of

An aerial view of Saipan, where Goerner believes Earhart was imprisoned by the Japanese. Goerner believes a massive government cover-up kept the public from hearing about Earhart's fate.

government bureaucracy is to keep delicate matters hidden until revealing them is absolutely necessary. In the first years after Earhart's disappearance, he argued, keeping her activities secret might have made real sense. After a while, though, keeping a lid on the affair simply became a matter of habit, routine, and inertia.

In Goerner's opinion, the cover-up was a disgrace to the nation. However, he also thought that Earhart and Noonan knew from the

Thomas E. Devine snips off the head of a dummy German soldier in this publicity shot. Devine believes that he saw the navy destroy Earhart's plane.

beginning that their mission would be dangerous and that government officials would deny all knowledge of their actions. They knew that if things went badly, they would be lost. "The most depressing aspect of the ordeal for both of them," Goerner wrote, "must have been the fact that their country could do nothing to rescue or ransom them."

The Burned Plane

One of the strangest theories about a government cover-up was constructed by Thomas E. Devine, who was a marine technical sergeant during and after the American occupation of the Pacific. In his 1987 book, *Eyewitness: The Amelia Earhart Incident*, he claims to have seen a startling event: the deliberate destruction of Earhart's plane by a team led by U.S. secretary of the navy James Forrestal. Devine never fully explained why Forrestal—or anyone else—would have wanted to destroy Earhart's plane. However, Devine's story is an unusual and intriguing one.

On his first day of being stationed on Saipan, Devine wrote, he noticed a twin-engine civilian airplane with the identifying marks NR16020—the same as Earhart's Electra—at Aslito airfield, the military air base on the island. He went back to his barracks and, while showering, heard a muffled explosion. He returned to the airfield and saw the same plane engulfed in flames. A number of military personnel stood nearby, watching passively.

Furthermore, Devine wrote, he was shocked to find later that the man who oversaw the plane's destruction—a mysterious figure in a white shirt —was none other than a top government official. Devine wrote:

> I realized that I could identify him. This mysterious man who personally supervised the security around NR16020 and apparently participated in its torching, the man in the white shirt, was Secretary of the Navy James Vincent Forrestal.

Devine offers no proof that this man was indeed Forrestal; presumably, he recognized him from photographs.

Previously, Devine had shown little interest in Earhart, but now he began to trace her trail. He was met with what he said was the first attempt to thwart his investigations by government officials. While Devine was following up a lead about Earhart's grave, a navy man approached him before the end of his tour of duty and tried to convince him to travel to Honolulu by air for "a briefing." The reason, Devine thought, was that he had been too curious about Earhart. Normally, Devine wrote, a marine sergeant like himself would have shipped home by sea at the end of his tour. He would have rated a trip by air only for extraordinary reasons. Suspecting a trap and unsure of what a briefing might have meant, Devine managed to avoid the navy man and obtained standard orders to return home.

Once back in the States, Devine claimed, the government harassment continued. On his way to interview Earhart's sister, Muriel, for instance, he stopped in a Boston restaurant and was served by a waitress. He claimed that later, while in the Hartford, Connecticut, branch of the Office of Naval Intelligence, he saw the same waitress again—and was shocked to discover that she was looking through a file on Amelia Earhart. He could only conclude that she had been following him. He also said that a mysterious

Allies invade Garapan, the capital of Saipan, during World War II. Did the navy cover up evidence of Earhart's landing and imprisonment on the island?

and strangely friendly cab driver followed him throughout his visit to Massachusetts. Devine became convinced that this man was also a government operative.

James Forrestal, the secretary of the navy whom Devine says deliberately destroyed Earhart's plane, met a sad and perhaps mysterious end. Forrestal died in 1949, just two months after resigning his post as America's first secretary of defense. He had been suffering from serious mental problems, and his death—he fell from a window at the naval hospital in Bethesda, Maryland—was officially declared suicide. Devine believed that Forrestal's death was not suicide at all, but was a highly suspicious part of a widespread government cover-up of the Earhart story.

Devine's inquiries, and those of others who have followed Earhart's trail, have produced as many intriguing questions as hard answers. The bottom line is that no one knows what really happened to Amelia Earhart. How she died, whether she was a spy, and charges of a government cover-up are all issues that may never be resolved.

 *Amelia Lives*

Nothing she might have said or done, no scheme George Palmer Putnam might have designed, could so enhance Earhart's renown as the mystery of her disappearance. She had been famous. By vanishing she became legendary.

Doris Rich, *Amelia Earhart*

Amelia Earhart has not lost any of her mystery or glamour over the years. Even today, researchers are devoting their lives to looking for new clues and spinning new theories about her.

One current investigator is Richard Gillespie, an American who heads The International Group for Historic Aircraft Recovery (TIGHAR). In 1989 and 1991, Gillespie mounted expeditions to Nikumaroro Island, a tiny atoll that is one of the Gilbert Islands. Nikumaroro, which is 420 miles southeast of Howland Island, was formerly known as Gardner Island.

On his first expeditions, Gillespie found what he thought was Earhart's grave, but it turned out to contain the remains of a native child. He also found a cigarette lighter and chart storage box that he thought might have belonged to Fred Noonan, but he was never able to prove his theory.

Then, in March 1992, Gillespie revealed what he believed was truly sensational evidence about Earhart.

Immediately after Earhart's disappearance, a navy seaplane had searched Gardner Island from the air. Lieutenant John O. Lambrecht, who flew that mission, reported seeing "signs of recent habitation," a phrase he used on other occasions to refer to native huts. He stated in his official report that he had not seen any evidence of an airplane or of distress signals. "Repeated circling and zooming," he said, "failed to elicit any answering wave from possible inhabitants and it was finally taken for granted that none were there."

The Lost Star

The name of the airplane that Amelia Earhart flew is an ironic one. In Greek mythology, Electra was one of the seven daughters of Atlas. Zeus changed them into stars so they could avoid pursuit by the hunter Orion, but Electra broke free and became a comet. This mythical figure has since been known as the Lost Star. It is also an appropriate name for history's most famous woman pilot.

Gillespie thought otherwise. He suggested that Earhart and Noonan were there. His chief piece of evidence was a scrap of corroded aluminum, measuring twenty-three inches by nineteen inches, that his team found on Nikumaroro. Gillespie said that the scrap matched the underbelly portion of Earhart's airplane's fuselage. At a 1992 press conference, Gillespie also displayed a Cat's Paw brand rubber heel from a size nine oxford-style shoe, found a quarter-mile inland among thick vegetation. A photo of Earhart taken days before her disappearance shows her wearing similar shoes.

A Tragic Emergency Crash

Furthermore, a length of copper aircraft radio antenna wire found on the island was identical to the type commonly used in the 1930s but obsolete by the time of the war. A cap from a bottle of antacid was another piece of Gillespie's evidence. Earhart, he noted, had been troubled with stomach problems throughout her flight.

"There is only one possible conclusion," Gillespie told the media: that Earhart and Noonan ventured off-course and, failing to find Howland, crash-landed on Gardner. Their plane was blown into the deep water surrounding Gardner and sunk by a tropical storm. The fliers lingered on the little island until they died of starvation and dehydration.

However, Elgen Long, a former airline pilot and a leading current authority on Earhart, has disputed Gillespie's findings. Shortly before the press conference, at Gillespie's request, Long had assembled a group of experts to examine the metal scrap. The group included an aircraft structures engineer, a metals engineering professor, owners of other Electra 10 airplanes, and the assistant foreman at the Lockheed shop at the time Earhart's plane was built.

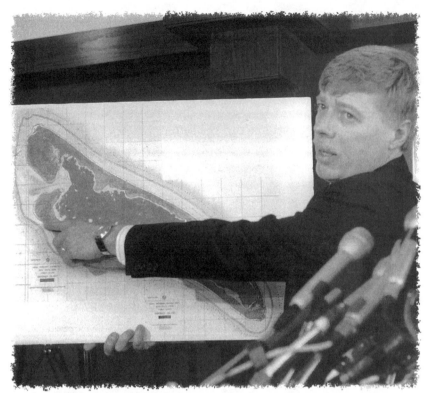

Richard Gillespie, head of The International Group for Historic Aircraft Recovery, points to the remote Pacific island of Nikumaroro where he believes Earhart landed and later perished.

This team examined archive photos, blueprints, sister planes, and even documents related to Earhart's crash in Hawaii. Its conclusion was that the metal scrap was not from Earhart's plane. "We decided the fragment could have come from anywhere," Long later commented. "Anywhere but Amelia Earhart's plane." He cited, among other discrepancies, differences in the spacing of the rivets and in certain pieces, called formers and stiffeners, that are used to strengthen an aircraft's frame.

Critics have also pointed out flaws in Gillespie's other pieces of evidence. Even tiny islands like Gardner were occupied by military personnel and natives during the war, which could account for the navy pilot's observation of inhabitants. Aluminum was a prized trade item to the Gilbertese, which might explain its presence there. The shoe heel, medicine bottle, cigarette lighter, and other artifacts could have come from anyone.

Gillespie remains undaunted, and the search goes on. Other researchers continue to scour government records and raise money

Amelia Remembered

In the months following Earhart's disappearance, dozens of memorials, such as scholarships, sprang up in her name. There is an Amelia Earhart Lane in Harrison, New York, an Earhart Road at the Oakland, California, airport, and an Earhart Street in her hometown of Atchison, Kansas. More than twenty cities have Earhart memorials and markers, and major displays honoring her can be found at Purdue University and the Smithsonian Institution, along with many smaller ones around the nation. Several schools have been named for her. As biographer Mary Love says in *The Sound of Wings:* "The ball that George [Putnam] had set rolling in 1928 had gathered speed by virtue of his publicity machine in the interim years and now—by an unfortunate accident—it had gathered its own momentum, which nothing and no one could stop."

Earhart Light on Howland Island is dedicated to the memory of Amelia Earhart.

to mount high-tech expeditions to the South Pacific. By using new technology, such as remote sensing, magnetic detection, sonar, and earth-penetrating radar, they expect to find more evidence to support their theories.

In the meantime, the public's fascination with the Amelia Earhart puzzle continues.

As the mystery deepens, Earhart's fame grows. Scholarship funds, airports, schools, and stadiums are named for her. The U.S.

Amelia Earhart continues to be remembered and revered as a pilot who did extraordinarily brave and daring things at a time when far less was expected of women.

Postal Service issued a stamp in her honor in 1964. The line of practical, lightweight luggage she designed and named for herself is still available. She is still the subject of frequent articles, television documentaries, and books. She even turns up occasionally in absurd supermarket tabloid headlines like this one: "Amelia Earhart Found Alive! She's 95 Years Old and Living on Tiny Island in South Pacific!"

An Inspiration

Amelia Earhart—strong, intelligent, unafraid to do things no woman had done before—also continues to serve as a positive role model for women. As biographer Mary Love put it, "It is impossible to evaluate the inspiration that Amelia handed down to the generations of women who came after her." In addition, she had an enormous impact on the aviation industry as a whole. Earhart and other pioneer aviators set new standards for the developing technology by demanding ever-better equipment. Often they paid the ultimate price, as did Earhart; but the airline industry of today is a direct result of their efforts.

Only a few days after Earhart's disappearance, newspaper columnist Walter Lippmann wrote these words:

> The world is a better place to live in because it contains human beings who will give up ease and security, and stake their own lives in order to do what they themselves think worth doing. . . . They do the useless, brave, noble, the divinely foolish and the very wisest things that are done by men. And what they prove to themselves and to others is that man is no mere creature of his habits, no mere automaton in his routine, no mere cog in the collective machine, but that in the dust of which he is made there is also fire, lighted now and then by the great winds from the sky.

No matter what Amelia Earhart's fate may have been, Lippmann's words still ring true. Even if Amelia Earhart died on a tropical morning in July 1937, she lives on.

For Further Reading

Melinda Blau, *Whatever Happened to Amelia Earhart?* Milwaukee: Raintree Books, 1977. Concentrates on Earhart's disappearance.

Patricia Lauber, *Lost Star: The Story of Amelia Earhart.* New York: Scholastic, 1988. A well-written biography.

Eileen Morey, *The Importance of Amelia Earhart.* San Diego, CA: Lucent Books, 1995. Concentrates on Earhart's life and adventures.

Blythe Randolph, *Amelia Earhart.* New York: Franklin Watts, 1987. A good introduction to Earhart's life.

Mary Dodson Wade, *Amelia Earhart: Flying for Adventure.* Brookfield, CT: Millbrook Press, 1992. An easy-to-read book about Earhart and her adventures.

Works Consulted

T. C. "Buddy" Brennan, *Witness to the Execution: The Odyssey of Amelia Earhart*. Frederick, CO: Renaissance House, 1988. The account of a Texas businessman's sleuthing into the Earhart mystery.

Paul L. Briand Jr., *Daughter of the Sky: The Story of Amelia Earhart*. New York: Duell, Sloan and Pearce, 1960. Written by a captain in the U.S. Air Force. First recounting of the story told by Josephine Blanco Akiyama.

Randall Brink, *Lost Star: The Search for Amelia Earhart*. New York: Norton, 1994. By a former pilot and aviation editor who claims to have uncovered a government plot to hide Earhart's spy mission.

Jackie Cochran, *The Stars at Noon*. Boston: Little, Brown, 1954. A memoir by a pioneer female aviator and Earhart's close friend.

Thomas E. Devine with Richard M. Daley, *Eyewitness: The Amelia Earhart Incident*. Frederick, CO: Renaissance House, 1987. Written by a man who believes he witnessed the destruction of Earhart's plane on Saipan in 1944.

Amelia Earhart, *Last Flight*. New York: Harcourt, Brace, 1937. Assembled by G. P. Putnam from notebooks written by A. E. and mailed back during her last flight.

Richard Gillespie, "You Mean, Nobody Really Looked in the Most Likely Place?" *Life*, April 1, 1992. By the man who claimed to have found evidence of Earhart's crash on Gardner Island.

Fred Goerner, *The Search for Amelia Earhart*. New York: Doubleday, 1966. A best-seller written by a CBS radio reporter who devoted many years to finding out what happened to A. E. Concludes that she was captured and executed by the Japanese.

Joe Klaas, *Amelia Earhart Lives*. New York: McGraw-Hill, 1970. Recounts the research of air force Major Joe Gervais and concludes that Earhart was smuggled out of occupied Japan after World War II in order to live under an assumed name in New Jersey.

Vincent V. Loomis with Jeffrey L. Ethell, *Amelia Earhart: The Final Story*. New York: Random House, 1985. A former air force officer claims to have found the wreckage of A. E.'s Electra while serving as operations officer on Eniwetok Atoll during the first H-bomb test in 1952.

Mary S. Love, *The Sound of Wings: The Life of Amelia Earhart.* New York: St. Martin's Press, 1989. The most thorough, detailed, and even-handed biography of A. E., and probably the best. Chooses not to speculate much on A. E.'s fate but presents summaries of various theories in an appendix. By the author of *Straight on Till Morning,* the life of pioneering woman aviator Beryl Markham.

Michael O'Leary, "The Earhart Controversy," *Air Progress,* July 1992. About Richard Gillespie's claims of Earhart evidence.

Ann Holtgren Pellegreno, *World Flight: The Earhart Trail.* Ames: Iowa State University Press, 1971. By a pilot who in 1967 traced Earhart's around-the-world flight in a similar airplane. Primarily a journal of that commemorative flight.

Doris L. Rich, *Amelia Earhart.* New York: Dell, 1989. A full biography, clearly and concisely written as part of the Smithsonian *History of Aviation* series. Concludes that Earhart and Noonan were not on a government mission and were lost at sea.

Susan Ware, *Still Missing: Amelia Earhart and the Search for Modern Feminism.* New York: W. W. Norton, 1993. A biography with a strong feminist viewpoint by a history professor at New York University.

Stephan Wilkinson, "Amelia Earhart: Is the Search Over?" *Smithsonian Air & Space,* August/September 1992. An article sympathetic to the findings of Richard Gillespie.

Donald Moyer Wilson, *Amelia Earhart: Lost Legend.* Webster, NY: Enigma Press, 1994. A compilation of stories, reports, and legends about Earhart by a former marine who served on Saipan during the Pacific invasion.

Video:

Nancy Porter (director/producer/writer): "Amelia Earhart." Boston: WGBH/PBS. An excellent video documentary originally made for *The American Experience* series, 1993.

Index

Akiyama, Josephine Blanco
  story of Earhart's disappear-
    ance, 59–61
Amaran, Billimon
  story of treating Noonan, 67
Amelia Earhart Foundation,
  54–55
Amelia Earhart, 10, 20, 58, 62
Amelia Earhart Lives, 72–73
Amelia Earhart: The Final Story,
  67

Balfour, Harry, 30
  comments on Earhart, 40
  radio contact with Earhart, 32
Bellarts, Leo G., 33
Blas, Nieves Cabrera
  story of Earhart's execution, 69
Bogan, Eugene
  story of Earhart's crash, 65
Bolam, Irene
  denial of link with Earhart,
    74–75
  speculation that she is Earhart,
    73–74
Brennan, T.C. "Buddy" (author
  of *Witness to the Execution*),
  69
  finds blindfold, 70
  theory that Earhart was exe-
    cuted, 69
Bresnik, Al, 25
Briand, Paul L., Jr. (author of
  Daughter of the Sky), 59
Brink, Randall (author of *Lost
  Star*), 79–80
  believes Earhart was alive until
    1937, 71–72, 73
  theory of Earhart as spy, 80–85
  thinks Earhart was captured,
    71
Brittain, M.L.
  theory of Earhart's disappear-
    ance, 48

Cochran, Jackie (author of *The
  Stars at Noon*), 45, 73

telepathic search for Earhart,
  45
Collins, Paul
  opinion on Earhart's disap-
    pearance, 53
Craig, Elliot, 57

Daughter of the Sky, 59
dead-stick landing, 39
Devine, Thomas E. (author of
  *Eyewitness: The Amelia
  Earhart Incident*), 70
  believes U.S. blew up Earhart's
    plane, 95
  harrassed by U.S. government,
    96–97
  story of Earhart's execution, 70

Earhart, Amelia
  around-the-world flight
    first leg of, 27–29
    plans for, 22
  as nurse's aide, 14
  as spy, 76–97
  as Tokyo Rose, 57–58
  childhood diseases, 13
  childhood of, 10–11, 12–14
  coast-to-coast flight of, 18
  disappearance of, 11
  first solo flights, 17
  first woman for transatlantic
    flight, 18–19
  hatred of fame, 10
  historical importance of, 10,
    103
  introduction to flying, 15–16
  lack of respect for radio equip-
    ment, 33
  likelihood of surviving plane
    crash, 39–40, 41
  marriage of, 20–21
  missing, 38
  parents' divorce and, 17
  participation in Women's Air
    Derby, 18–19
  rising career, 21
  rumors of execution of, 52

rumors of Japanese capture,
50–52
rumors of participation in spy
mission, 48
search called off, 46
Earhart, Amy (mother)
believes daughter flew for government, 52
reaction to disappearance, 44
Earhart, Edwin (father), 12–13
alcoholism of, 14
Earhart, Muriel (sister), 13
investigation of spy rumors, 53
Electra 10E
Earhart's airplane, 21
Earhart's problems with, 27
may have been over weight
limit, 30, 32
Ellis, Earl, 49
*Eyewitness: The Amelia Earhart
Incident*, 70

Flight for Freedom (movie),
76–77
Forrestal, James, 95, 97

Gervais, Joseph
concludes that Earhart was a
spy, 86–87
theory that Irene Bolam is
Earhart, 73–74
Gillespie, Richard,
theory of Earhart's disappearance, 98–100
Goerner, Fred (author of *The
Search for Amelia Earhart*),
24, 61–63
government attempts to block
research, 89–95
investigation of bones, 91–92
organizes search of Tanapag
Harbor, 64
search for Earhart's and Noonan's grave, 64
theories of
Earhart as spy, 77–78
Earhart's death on Saipan, 66
larger engines on Earhart's
plane, 78–79
Gordon, Slim, 17
Gurr, Joseph

comments on Earhart's radio
equipment, 26

Howland Island, 17
difficulties of flight to, 29–30
Itasca, 29
radio contact with Earhart,
34–36

Japan
denial that it found Earhart, 50
planning for war, 47, 48
Jibambam, Elieu
story of Earhart's crash, 64–65
Johnson, Kelly Clarence, 53–54

Klaas, Joe, 51, 72–73

Lindbergh, Charles
historic flight of, 17
Loomis, Victor
theories of
Earhart not a spy, 86–87
Earhart's capture and death,
68–69
Earhart's crash, 66–67
Japanese lied to U.S., 89
Los Angeles, 15
Lost Star, 79–80
Love, Mary (author of *The
Sound of Wings*), 38, 55, 57
belief in Putnam's love of
Earhart, 56, 57
believes that Earhart crashed,
60
doubts about Earhart's capture, 52

Mahan, John
story of Earhart's crash, 64
Mantz, Paul, 24–25, 53
instructions on crashing plane
at sea, 39
McCown, Theodore
examines Earhart's supposed
skeleton, 64
McKneely, Bo, 27
McMenamy, Walter, 84–85

New Guinea
last place Earhart seen, 29

Noonan, Fred (navigator for around-the-world flight), 11, 23, 32
difficulties in navigation, 29–30, 31

Operation Earhart, 51
conclusions that Earhart was a spy, 86–87

Palmer, Cap, 58
theory of Earhart as spy, 76–77
Pangelinan, José
story of Earhart's grave, 63
Pearl Harbor, 48
Price, Willard, 49
Putnam, George Palmer, 18
continued search for Earhart, 45–46, 55
proposal to Earhart, 19–20
radio contact with Earhart, 32
reaction to Earhart's disappearance, 42, 44

radio contact
loss of, 33
radio equipment
Earhart's lack of, 26–27
lack of knowledge about Earhart's, 38
problems with transmission, 40
Rafford, Paul, Jr., 67
Rich, Doris (author of *Amelia Earhart*), 10, 20, 30, 37, 62
describing Earhart's shyness, 58
Roosevelt, Franklin and Eleanor, 21
deny Earhart's spy involvement, 52–53

order military to search for Earhart, 41
reaction to Earhart's disappearance, 44

San Nicolas, Matilde
story of Earhart's capture, 61–63
Schlesinger, Arthur, Jr., 52–53
Search for Amelia Earhart, The, 24
Smith, Elinor, 21
Snook, Neta (Earhart's first flying teacher), 16
Sound of Wings, The, 57, 60
Stars at Noon, The, 45
Still Missing, 43
Stultz, Bill, 17
Sugita, Michiko
story of Earhart's execution, 70

Thompson, Warren K., 32, 36
initiates search for Earhart, 41
Tokyo Rose
Earhart as, 57–58
Truman, Harry
cover-up of Earhart's spy involvement, 92–93

Vidal, Gore, 58

Washburn, Bradford
criticism of Earhart, 43
Ware, Susan (author of *Still Missing*), 43
Witness to the Execution: The Odyssey of Amelia Earhart, 69
Women's Air Derby, 18–19
World War I, 14
Wright, Wilbur and Orville, 14

Picture Credits

Cover photo, clockwise from left: Smithsonian Institution, AP/Wide World Photos, Smithsonian Institution,

AP/Wide World Photos, 24, 42, 61, 65, 66, 82, 86, 93

Archive Photos, 80, 96, 101

Library of Congress, 11, 19, 49, 51, 53

National Archives, 41

Ninety-Nines Library, 20

Radcliffe College, 12, 13, 15, 16, 39, 54, 56, 84, 102

REUTERS/Mike Theiler/Archive Photos, 100

Smithsonian Institution, 23, 25, 26, 28, 34, 62

UN Photo, 45

UPI/Corbis-Bettmann, 31, 48, 63, 70, 72, 74, 78, 83, 90, 94

About the Author

Adam Woog is the author of several books for adults and young people. For Lucent Books, he has written *The U.N.*, *The Importance of Harry Houdini*, *The Importance of Louis Armstrong*, *The Importance of Duke Ellington*, and *Poltergeists*. He lives with his wife and daughter in Seattle, Washington.